THE
BALANCED DIET
COOKBOOK

**EASY MENUS AND RECIPES FOR COMBINING
CARBOHYDRATES, PROTEINS, AND FATS**

BILL TAYLOR

**THE CROSSING PRESS
FREEDOM, CALIFORNIA**

For information on bulk purchases or group discounts for this and other Crossing Press titles, please contact our Special Sales Manager at 800/777-1048.

Visit our Web site on the Internet: www.crossingpress.com

Library of Congress Cataloging-in-Publication Data

Taylor, Bill (Robert William)
    The balanced diet cookbook: easy menus and recipes for combining carbohydrates, proteins, and fats / Bill Taylor.
        p. cm.
    Includes index.
    ISBN 0-89594-874-5 (paper)
    1. Reducing diets–Recipes 2. Food combining 3. Nutrition.
I. Title.
  RM222.2.T36 1997
  641.5'63–dc21   97-24528
                                                                  CIP

CONTENTS

BILL'S STORY

In 1969 Bill Taylor landed by accident in the restaurant business. Out of work and desperate with his wife six months pregnant, he took a job two nights a week washing dishes in a steak house in Santa Cruz. Two years later he was managing the place. Fours years later he founded his own restaurant and became still more interested in food preparation, spending hours in the kitchen with his chefs, asking questions, watching them work, and asking for their secrets. In fact, he became so interested he went back to school to learn more about the culinary arts.

In 1993, Elaine Gill, publisher of The Crossing Press, asked Bill to design and operate a kitchen for her new office building. She wanted a place where people could have hot oatmeal in the morning along with coffee and toast plus a hot meal at lunch— a place where they could talk together and just hang out. She also wanted a kitchen where new ideas for cookbooks could be tried out and recipes tested. Almost all the recipes in this collection were developed in the Crossing Press kitchen, then eaten and judged by eager participants.

INTRODUCTION

Just a little over a year ago my dentist discovered that I had some unusual cells in my mouth and warned me that at any time they could turn cancerous. At the time I was smoking two packs of cigarettes a day, spending most of the late afternoon and early evening lounging around in front of the TV, eating everything in sight. I was carrying 195 pounds on a 5'8" frame. I couldn't get up a flight of stairs without losing my breath. I was pushing fifty and realized that if I didn't make some big changes in my life soon, there might not be that much time left.

I enrolled in a Quit Smoking class at the local hospital and went to every class. In this particular program there were people in different stages, some newcomers like me, others who had not smoked in six months. The one piece of advice they gave me was the importance of exercise. So I started walking a little everyday, along the beach. Soon, I started to see how fast I could walk this route. There is a long flight of stairs leading down to the beach from the top of the cliffs, and I began to run up and down them several times a day. By this time I was working out fairly hard, but my body didn't seem to be changing that much. I felt better and had gotten some of my wind back. I wasn't sitting in front of the television all afternoon, but I couldn't seem to be able to lose the extra weight.

A friend told me about a book with a new idea on combining foods. I felt it might be worth checking into, so I picked up a copy of *Enter the Zone* by Barry Sears. It soon became clear that I had never considered the consequence of the food I was eating; I didn't have a planned diet. After finishing Sears's book I realized that I needed to pay more attention to my carbohydrate-protein-fat ratio.

I weighed myself, figured out my lean body mass-to-fat ratio, and how many blocks I needed at each meal. I then started eating as many balanced meals as I could. On that first day, even though I had been exercising regularly for several months, I weighed 196 pounds and had a lean body mass-to-fat ratio of more than 7 percent over the national average. In just four months following the Zone regimen I weighed in at 163, was down two pants sizes, and my fat to lean body mass was 3 percent lower than the national average for males my age. Since that time I added weights as part of my weekly routine, and by now have put a little weight back on. But I'm still down to size 31 pants and my fat to lean body mass ratio has remained the same. Needless to say, I'm a believer.

When I first started eating balanced meals I was never sure if I had the carbohydrate-to-protein-to-fat ratio right. Most of the recipes I found in the Zone literature or on the Internet didn't make much sense to me. I figured that if I was having trouble it could be a nightmare for some people. Many combinations created to balance a meal didn't sound appetizing. One woman I know was eating cereal, sardines, and nuts for breakfast; another was eating ice cream, cream cheese, and avocado for lunch.

I started searching the bookstores for information and was coming up blank. I decided I needed to develop some recipes using real food for real people, primarily for me.

This book was put together to help people who already are following a balanced meal plan advocated by Sears, but who are looking for some extra help. I'm not interested in convincing anyone that this is the way to live. What I'm doing here is preaching to the people who are already converted. If you have any doubts or questions or if you need further information, I suggest that you read Sears's book.

In the meanwhile here are some suggestions I've picked up along the way that may be helpful:

▶ Calculate your lean body mass-to-fat ratio and update it on a monthly basis.

▶ Blocks are food groups. One block of carbohydrate is 9 grams. One block of protein is 7 grams. One block of fat is 3 grams.

▶ Be sure at the end of the day that you have consumed all the protein blocks you need for that day.

▶ Never consume fewer than 8 protein blocks a day no matter what your protein requirements are.

▶ Be sure to eat one hour after waking and never go more than five hours without another meal, hungry or not.

- ▶ Afternoon and late night snacks are critical to a balanced food plan. Don't skip them, even if you are not hungry.

- ▶ Focus on complex carbohydrates such as fruits and vegetables. You can eat undesirable carbohydrates, such as breads, pasta, starches, and grains, but in smaller amounts.

- ▶ Use primarily monounsaturated fat, such as olive oil or canola oil.

- ▶ Drink a lot of water, at least 8 ounces during the day, with every meal and every snack, and several more glasses between meals.

- ▶ Exercise, exercise, exercise! Nothing will change without a regular workout program.

- ▶ Eat oatmeal at least three times a week for the GLA (gamma linolenic acid). Eat salmon or tuna at least three times a week for the EPA (eicosapentaenoic acid).

How to Use This Cookbook

I have included a six-week meal planner to help you with your meals and your shopping list. You may want to design your own chart, taking into account what you like to eat, what you have left over, what is fresh in the market, etc. I found it easier to think things out and make a plan ahead of time.

The recipes are arranged in four sections, breakfast, lunch, dinner, and snacks. I have included dishes in those groups that people like myself normally associate with a particular meal: eggs for breakfast, sandwiches for lunch, and so on. Not all the recipes are balanced. If not, I have suggested ways on how to achieve that goal. For those of you striking out on your own for the first time, remember to keep the carbohydrate and protein blocks in a 1 to 1 ratio. I also included information on some ingredients I use in balanced cooking, on ways to make them work well, and on some of the problems I encountered.

In October 1996 the American Heart Association raised the fat content of their recommended diet to at least 15 percent. For years the association had advised no more than 10 percent fat, with 5 percent being even better. So even this conservative association is starting to understand the importance of more fat in meals.

Be warned that hard cheeses and some soft cheeses have a fat content that can equal the protein content per gram and sometimes exceed it. I suggest that when you are using hard cheeses, reduce the fat from other parts of the recipe wherever possible.

There is some debate about whether a fat block is 3 grams or 1.5 grams. With some protein sources there is a crossover between fat and protein, especially for meats, poultry, seafood, and cheeses. I have calculated 1.5 grams of fat in a block when cooking with these proteins, and 3 grams of fat in a block when cooking with other sources, such as protein powders. I'm fairly certain of one thing: If you are going to make a mistake, err in the direction of the proteins and fats, not the carbohydrates.

I've tried to standardize the measurements as much as possible, but at times it was unavoidable, and I had to change from tablespoons to grams and ounces. There is no such measurement as ⅓ teaspoon. I use the measurement of a rounded ¼ teaspoon in its place. For liquid measurements that call for a ⅓ teaspoon I've indicated ¼+ teaspoons, to indicate that you need a little splash over to make up the measurement.

Always salt and pepper the dishes to your taste. I know that some people like to eat low-sodium foods, and I felt it was presumptuous for me to be salting their food. When a recipe does call for a specific measurement of salt and pepper, it is an important part of the recipe.

I have arranged the recipes in the order I liked. That doesn't mean you couldn't use a snack for breakfast, or a lunch recipe for dinner.

Good luck with your food plan. I hope you succeed.

Special Ingredients and Preferences

Here is a list of some special ingredients. Today, supermarkets cater to diverse cultural influences and most everything you need can be purchased there. Some larger stores even have health food sections where natural products can be purchased. However, in such stores, an item may be limited to one brand, not always the best one available. So find a good natural foods or Asian market in order to do some comparative shopping.

Almond Butter
This product is sold in most natural food stores and some supermarkets. It has a nutty flavor and the consistency of peanut butter. Stir it before using, as the oil rises to the top.

Balsamic Vinegar
This Italian vinegar, found in all supermarkets, is made from white grapes and aged for several years in wood barrels to give it a dark brown color and a mellow, sweet-and-sour taste. The best balsamic vinegars are carefully aged for decades and are extremely expensive.

Breads and Rolls
I buy a good quality whole wheat bread from a bakery because I like the taste and don't want a lot of chemicals in my food. In a balanced food plan, your stomach doesn't know the difference between a commercial white bread and a good quality whole wheat bread, but my mouth and my mind do.

Rye breads on the other hand have a smaller impact on the carbohydrate load than other types of breads. Use them whenever possible.

Dairy Products
The most balanced milk you can buy contains 2% fat. When using sour cream and yogurt always buy the low-fat brands. Because there is some crossover between carbohydrates and protein in dairy products, the reduced fat brings the product closer to the center. Eliminating the fat pushes the product to the outer edge of the food plan.

Canola Mayonnaise
Found in natural food stores, canola mayonnaise is made from canola oil and corn starch. The flavor is a little lemony, but other

than that it resembles mayonnaise both in taste and texture. The light version has only 3 grams of fat per tablespoon.

Fish Sauce

A product of Thailand, this sauce can be found in the Asian section of most supermarkets, or in Asian markets. This sauce is made from anchovies, water, and salt. It has a extremely potent flavor, but blends nicely as a seasoning when cooked.

Garam Masala

Commercial garam masala is available in stores specializing in East Indian food stuffs. I haven't seen this mixture of spices in supermarkets yet. Most Indian cooks mix their own spices daily, using garam masala the same way Western cooks use salt and pepper. (See page 12 for my recipe).

Hoisin Sauce

The Chinese use this sauce for dipping and seasoning. It's fairly common in most supermarkets, or an Asian market. It's a jam-like sauce made from fermented soy beans, sweet and bitter with a spicy aftertaste.

Oyster Sauce

Like Hoisin sauce, oyster sauce is readily available in most supermarkets and all Asian markets. Oyster sauce is made from dried oysters, soy sauce, and brine. The best sauces are fermented for years. This sauce has a salty flavor, so you may want to eliminate additional salt.

Protein Powder

It is made from specially curdled milk. It can be purchased in most health food and natural foods stores. Protein powder can be mixed into drinks, or used for cooking and baking. I usually buy a name brand, but you can also purchase it in bulk in natural food stores.

Salad Dressing

I use Kraft Free Italian or Kraft Free Caesar on salads. Both dressings contain one gram of fat or protein, and only three grams carbohydrate per two tablespoonfuls. Or if you prefer, use fresh lemon juice or vinegar on your salad. I've found that homemade dressings contain way too much fat and can upset the balance of your meal.

Sesame Oil

There are two varieties, the light and dark sesame oils. The light oil is extruded from raw seeds. It is used for sautéing and stir fries, and baked goods that require a light, fragrant oil. The dark oil is made from toasted seeds. The flavor of this oil is far more intense than the light oil. It is used in marinades, in anything that requires a strong taste.

The light oil is available in health food stores. It is somewhat hard to find in supermarkets. The dark oil is available in Asian markets, some supermarkets, and health food stores.

Tahini

A staple in Mid-Eastern cooking, tahini is a oily paste made from crushed sesame seeds. Western cooks will find it readily available in most supermarkets or natural foods stores. Like almond butter it separates easily and should be stirred before using.

Tofu

Made from soybeans, tofu is a key protein source for millions of people. Its texture is smooth and silky. The flavor is bland, but it picks up other flavors readily. You can find it in almost all supermarkets in the fresh vegetable section. However, you will find the best selection of tofu is in natural foods stores. Look for firm, soft, or whipped.

Whey Protein Powder

Whey protein is derived from the watery part of milk. It is higher in protein grams than protein powder per serving and tends to blend well in cooking and baking. Find it in all natural foods stores either commercially packaged or in bulk.

Basic Recipes and Procedures

Here are some recipes for items that I use frequently. Most can be made days ahead of time and stored in tightly sealed containers in the pantry or refrigerator.

CURRY POWDER

2 teaspoons ground turmeric
4 teaspoons ground cumin
8 teaspoons cayenne
16 teaspoons ground coriander

▶ Mix all the ingredients together and store in an airtight jar.

GARAM MASALA

1 tablespoon black peppercorns
16 cloves
3 teaspoons ground cardamom
2 teaspoon ground cinnamon
1 teaspoon black cumin seeds
2 teaspoon cumin seeds
2 bay leaves

▶ Add all the ingredients to a coffee grinder or pepper mill and grind down to a powder. Store in an airtight jar.

GUACAMOLE

1/2 cup yogurt cheese (page 15)
1 ripe avocado, skin and seed removed
1 tablespoon fresh lime juice
1 tomato, peeled, seeded, and chopped
2 tablespoons chopped red onion
2 tablespoons chopped fresh cilantro
1 fresh jalapeño chili, seeded and minced
2 tablespoons whey protein powder
Salt and pepper

▶ Add all the ingredients to a food processor or blender and mix until smooth. Cover and chill at least two hours before using. Seal tightly and refrigerate for several days.

½ tablespoon = 1 fat block

ROASTED GARLIC

3 whole heads garlic
1 tablespoon olive oil
1 teaspoon butter
2 tablespoons water

▶ Preheat the oven to 325° F.

▶ Slice the tops from the heads of the garlic and trim the base so the garlic will sit flat. Remove some of the outer skin from the garlic but do not separate the cloves. Place the garlic in a small baking dish, and drizzle each with some of the olive oil. Dot the garlic with some butter and drizzle with the water. Cover the dish with foil or a lid, and bake for 75 minutes. Remove the lid and bake for an additional 15 minutes. Cool before using.

Each head of garlic = 1 block carbohydrate, protein, and fat.

ROASTED PEPPERS

▶ To roast peppers, turn the stove to high heat. Place the peppers directly in the flame. Turn with tongs several times until the whole outer skin of the pepper has been blackened, about 5 minutes. Remove from the flame and put into a paper bag for 15 minutes to steam. Cool and remove the blackened skin. Cut in half and remove the membrane and seeds.

STOCKS

▶ Most of the stocks called for in this book are made from chicken, beef, or vegetables. I usually buy canned stocks for convenience. Bouillon cubes which have no impact on a balanced food plan are another easy way to prepare stock. If you are using a commercial beef or chicken stock, buy either a non-fat variety, or strain the fat out of the stock right after opening the can. For those who want to make their own, here's a versatile vegetable stock.

VEGETABLE STOCK

Trimmings from vegetables
4 cloves garlic, chopped
2 tablespoons olive oil
1 cup dry sherry
8 cups water
3 bay leaves
1 teaspoon dried basil
1 teaspoon dried oregano
Salt and pepper

▶ Preheat the oven to 400° F.

▶ Save all the trimmings and peelings from any vegetable you have used recently. Add all the trimmings and garlic to a roasting pan. Drizzle with the olive oil and bake for 45 minutes, turning every 10 minutes. Place the roasting pan on the stove top over a high heat and add the dry sherry. Bring to a boil and cook until the liquid has evaporated. Add the water, bay leaves, basil, oregano, and salt and pepper, and return to a boil.

▶ Reduce the heat and simmer until the liquid has reduced by half. Strain the stock through cheese cloth and discard the vegetables. Adjust the seasoning. The stock can be stored in a tightly sealed container in the refrigerator for several weeks.

SPICY SALSA

2 tomatoes, diced
1 small onion, diced
2 cloves garlic, minced
1 tablespoon jalapeño, seeded and chopped
1/3 cup minced, fresh cilantro
1 teaspoon dried oregano
1/2 teaspoon cayenne, more or less
1 tablespoon fresh lime juice
Salt and pepper

▶ Put all the ingredients into a food processor or blender. Pulse 2 or 3 times until blended well, but still chunky. This will keep covered in the refrigerator for several days.

This recipe = 5 blocks carbohydrates

TAHINI SAUCE

2 teaspoons olive oil
1 tablespoon tahini
1/2 teaspoon balsamic vinegar
1 scallion, chopped

▶ Combine all the ingredients in a blender or food processor. Pulse until well mixed. I like to make a cup or two at a time, and use it as I need it. Cover and refrigerate for up to two weeks.

YOGURT CHEESE

▶ Line a colander with a couple of layers of cheesecloth and place it over a bowl. Spoon the yogurt into the colander and let it drip overnight. Discard the drippings. The yogurt will be as thick as cream cheese and slightly more tart. It can be stored in its original container in the refrigerator for several weeks.

Weekly Menu Planner

Following is a six-week meal plan based on the recipes in this book. Each meal has been carefully blocked out to combine the carbohydrates, protein, and fat required in a balanced food plan. This is intended as a guide only: you should feel free to choose the meals that suit your present needs. Each meal is based on a requirement of four to five blocks for breakfast, lunch, and dinner, and two blocks for snacks.

WEEK ONE

SUNDAY

Breakfast . . . . . .Huevos Rancheros Omelet, page 34
Lunch . . . . .Greek Salad, page 84
Snack . . . . .Chive Popovers, page 143
Dinner . . . . .Broiled Salmon with a Mustard
                  Vinaigrette, page 122
Snack . . . . .Crustless Pumpkin Pie, page 149

MONDAY

Breakfast . . . . . .Perfectly Balanced Oatmeal, page 29
Lunch . . . . .Chicken Salad Pita, page 70
Snack . . . . .Homemade 40-30-30 Bar, page 158
Dinner . . . . .Chicken with a Lemon-Basil Sauce,
                  page 111
Snack . . . . .Crustless Pumpkin Pie, page 149

TUESDAY

Breakfast . . . . . .Bagel, Cream Cheese, and Lox, page 67
Lunch . . . . .Lunchtime Quesadilla, page 77
Snack . . . . .Chive Popovers, page 143
Dinner . . . . .Pork and Red Chili Stir-Fry, page 104
Snack . . . . .Chocolate Pudding Snack, page 150

WEDNESDAY

Breakfast . . . . . .Perfectly Balanced Oatmeal, page 29
Lunch . . . . .BLT and Cheese Sandwich, page 58
Snack . . . . .Homemade 40-30-30 Bar, page 158
Dinner . . . . .One-Skillet Beef Stew, page 92
Snack . . . . .Crustless Pumpkin Pie, page 149

THURSDAY

Breakfast ......Mushroom Scramble, page 46
Lunch ....Broiled Tofu Pita, page 71
Snack ....Curry Dip with Crackers, page 132
Dinner ....Baked Salmon with Tomatoes, Olives, and
　　　　　　　　　　Fresh Herbs, page 121
Snack ....Chocolate Pudding Snack, page 150

FRIDAY

Breakfast ......Egg Muffin, page 41
Lunch ....Chicken Fajitas, page 78
Snack ....Bagel, Lox, and Avocado (see one-block
　　　　　　　　　　snack chart, page 159)
Dinner ....Garlic-Roasted Chicken, page 115
Snack ....Curry Dip with Crackers, page 132

SATURDAY

Breakfast ......Perfectly Balanced Oatmeal, page 29
Lunch ....Balanced Minestrone Soup, page 87
Snack ....Peanut Butter-Oatmeal Cookies,
　　　　　　　　　　page 146
Dinner ....Pork Scaloppine, page 102
Snack ....Peanut Butter-Oatmeal Cookies,
　　　　　　　　　　page 146

WEEK TWO

SUNDAY

Breakfast ......Italian Omelet, page 37
Lunch ....Grilled Chicken and Cheese Sandwich, page 60
Snack ....Fresh Herb Dip with Crackers, page 131
Dinner ....Steak with a Mustard Peppercorn Sauce, page 95
Snack ....Yogurt with Nuts (see one-block snack chart, page 159)

MONDAY

Breakfast ......Bagel with Salmon Spread, page 63
Lunch ....Tofu Pita Sandwich, page 75
Snack ....Spice Cookies, page 147
Dinner ....Baked Halibut with Red Peppers and Red Onion, page 118
Snack ....Spice Cookies, page 147

TUESDAY

Breakfast ......Perfectly Balanced Oatmeal, page 29
Lunch ....Egg Salad Sandwich, page 61
Snack ....Commerical balanced bar
Dinner ....Chicken with Fresh Basil and Olives, page 110
Snack ....Banana-Nut Muffins, page 152

WEDNESDAY

Breakfast ......Cottage Cheese Omelet, page 35
Lunch ....Balsamic Yogurt Salad, page 82
Snack ....Banana-Nut Muffins, page 152
Dinner ....Scallops with Walnuts and Shallots, page 125
Snack ....Balanced Brownies, page 157

THURSDAY

Breakfast . . . . . .Perfectly Balanced Oatmeal, page 29
Lunch . . . . .Better Than Tuna Sandwich, page 62
Snack . . . . .Homemade 40-30-30 Bar, page 158
Dinner . . . . .Peppers and Beef Stir-Fry, page 94
Snack . . . . .Balanced Brownies, page 157

FRIDAY

Breakfast . . . . . .Bill's Fast Breakfast, page 30
Lunch . . . . .BLT and Cheese Sandwich, page 58
Snack . . . . .Oatmeal-Raisin Cookies, page 145
Dinner . . . . .Red Snapper Stew, page 123
Snack . . . . .Oatmeal-Raisin Cookies, page 145

SATURDAY

Breakfast . . . . . .Perfectly Balanced Oatmeal, page 29
Lunch . . . . .Chicken and Cucumber Chatt, page 72
Snack . . . . .Melon and Lox, page 142
Dinner . . . . .Spicy Stuffed Peppers, page 98
Snack . . . . .Pumpkin Muffins, page 154

WEEK THREE

SUNDAY

Breakfast ......Crustless Classic Quiche, page 49
Lunch ....Spinach and Fennel with Tarragon
              Dressing, page 85
Snack ....Pumpkin Muffins, page 154
Dinner ....Broiled Salmon with a Mustard
              Vinaigrette, page 122
Snack ....Oatmeal-Raisin Cookies, page 145

MONDAY

Breakfast ......Perfectly Balanced Oatmeal, page 29
Lunch ....Mediterranean Tuna Pita, page 73
Snack ....Fruit, Cheese, and Nuts (see one-block
              snack chart, page 159)
Dinner ....Szechuan Chicken, page 112
Snack ....Pumpkin Muffins, page 154

TUESDAY

Breakfast ......Bagel, Cream Cheese, and Lox, page 67
Lunch ....Salmon Pizza Bread, page 66
Snack ....Homemade 40-30-30 Bar, page 158
Dinner ....Halibut Provencale, page 120
Snack ....Almond Sugar Cookies, page 144

WEDNESDAY

Breakfast ......Perfectly Balanced Oatmeal, page 29
Lunch ....Beef and Vegetable Soup, page 88
Snack ....Berries, Cottage Cheese, and Nuts
.... (see one-block snack chart, page 159)
Dinner ....Keema Mater (Indian Spiced Beef),
              page 99
Snack ....Almond Sugar Cookies, page 144

THURSDAY

Breakfast . . . . . .Cottage Cheese and Mixed Fruit, page 32
Lunch . . . . .Turkey and Bacon Sandwich, page 59
Snack . . . . .Homemade 40-30-30 Bar, page 158
Dinner . . . . . . .Chicken with a Mushroom-Sherry Sauce,
                   page 114
Snack . . . . .Chocolate Pudding Snack, page 150

FRIDAY

Breakfast . . . . . .Strawberries and Crepes, page 53
Lunch . . . . .Red Lentil and Parmesan Pita, page 74
Snack . . . . .Ginger Tofu Dip with Crackers, page 133
Dinner . . . . . . .Linguine with Hot Shrimp and Asparagus,
                   page 124
Snack . . . . .Yogurt and Nuts (see one-block
                   snack chart, page 159)

SATURDAY

Breakfast . . . . . .Perfectly Balanced Oatmeal, page 29
Lunch . . . . .Tossed Broccoli and Cauliflower Salad,
                   page 86
Snack . . . . .Homemade 40-30-30 Bar, page 158
Dinner . . . . . . .Pork Tenderloin in a White Wine Sauce,
                   page 103
Snack . . . . .Chocolate Pudding Snack, page 150

WEEK FOUR

SUNDAY

Breakfast . . . . . . .French Toast and Bacon, page 51
Lunch . . . . .Tunisian Pita with Avocado, page 76
Snack . . . . .Homemade 40-30-30 Bar, page 158
Dinner . . . . . . .Baked Salmon with Tomatoes, Olives, and
                            Fresh Herbs, page 121
Snack . . . . .Balanced Brownies, page 157

MONDAY

Breakfast . . . . . .Breakfast Quesadilla, page 43
Lunch . . . . .Balanced Chili Beans, page 97
Snack . . . . .Yogurt and Nuts (see one-block
                            snack chart, page 159)
Dinner . . . . .Pan-Grilled Steak and Mushrooms,
                            page 90
Snack . . . . .Balanced Brownies, page 157

TUESDAY

Breakfast . . . . . .Perfectly Balanced Oatmeal, page 29
Lunch . . . . .Indian Carrot and Cucumber Salad,
                            page 80
Snack . . . . .Homemade 40-30-30 Bar, page 158
Dinner . . . . . . .Orange-Ginger Chicken, page 107
Snack . . . . .Banana Bread, page 156

WEDNESDAY

Breakfast . . . . . .Bagel with Salmon Spread, page 63
Lunch . . . . .Tofu Fajitas, page 79
Snack . . . . .Chive Popovers, page 143
Dinner . . . . .Penne with Scallops in a Tomato-
                            Vodka Sauce, page 127
Snack . . . . .Spice Cookies, page 147

THURSDAY

Breakfast . . . . . .Perfectly Balanced Oatmeal, page 29
Lunch . . . . .BLT Pita, page 69
Snack . . . . .Melon and Lox, page 142
Dinner . . . . .Peppers and Beef Stir-Fry, page 94
Snack . . . . .Banana Bread, page 156

FRIDAY

Breakfast . . . . . .Hearty Scrambled Eggs with Sausage and
                 Thyme, page 40
Lunch . . . . .Salami and Sun-Dried Tomato
                 Pizza Bread, page 65
Snack . . . . .Homemade 40-30-30 Bar, page 158
Dinner . . . . .Baked Halibut and Yogurt, page 117
Snack . . . . .Banana Bread, page 156

SATURDAY

Breakfast . . . . . .Perfectly Balanced Oatmeal, page 29
Lunch . . . . .Chicken Salad Sandwich, page 57
Snack . . . . .Chive Popovers, page 143
Dinner . . . . .Stir-Fry Chicken Hoisin, page 105
Snack . . . . .Spice Cookies, page 147

WEEK FIVE

SUNDAY

Breakfast ......All-American Cheese Omelet, page 33
Lunch ....Philly Cheese Pizza Bread, page 64
Snack ....Crackers, Cheese, and Sour Cream
       (see one-block snack chart, page 159)
Dinner ....Beef Burgundy, page 91
Snack ....Peanut Butter-Oatmeal Cookies,
       page 146

MONDAY

Breakfast ......Yogurt for Breakfast, page 31
Lunch ....Tomato with Cucumber-Macadamia Nut
       Salad, page 81
Snack ....Homemade 40-30-30 Bar, page 158
Dinner ....Broiled Salmon with a Mustard
       Vinaigrette, page 122
Snack ....Chocolate Pudding Snack, page 150

TUESDAY

Breakfast ......Perfectly Balanced Oatmeal, page 29
Lunch ....Egg Salad Sandwich, page 61
Snack ....Homemade 40-30-30 Bar, page 158
Dinner ....Honey-Soy Chicken, page 108
Snack ....Peanut Butter-Oatmeal Cookies,
       page 146

WEDNESDAY

Breakfast ......Egg and Sausage Muffin, page 42
Lunch ....Bagel with Salmon Spread Sandwich,
       page 63
Snack ....Crackers, Beef Jerky, and Avocado
       (see one-block snack chart, page 159)
Dinner ....Pork Amandine, page 106
Snack ....Peanut Butter-Oatmeal Cookies,
       page 146

THURSDAY

Breakfast ......Perfectly Balanced Oatmeal, page 29
Lunch ....Roasted Red Pepper Salad with Tarragon
                Vinaigrette, page 83
Snack ....Homemade 40-30-30 Bar, page 158
Dinner ....Seared Sea Scallops with Saffron,
                page 129
Snack ....Chocolate Pudding Snack, page 150

FRIDAY

Breakfast ......Blintzes with Blueberries, page 55
Lunch ....Greek Salad, page 84
Snack ....Berries, Yogurt, and Nuts (see one-block
                snack chart, page 159)
Dinner ....Garlic-Roasted Chicken, page 115
Snack ....Banana-Nut Muffins, page 152

SATURDAY

Breakfast ......Mushroom Scramble, page 46
Lunch ....Broiled Tofu Pita, page 71
Snack ....Bagel, Lox, and Sour Cream
                (see one-block snack chart, page 159)
Dinner ....One-Skillet Beef Stew, page 92
Snack ....Banana-Nut Muffins, page 152

WEEK SIX

SUNDAY

Breakfast . . . . . .Perfectly Balanced Oatmeal, page 29
Lunch . . . . .Chicken Salad Pita, page 70
Snack . . . . .Berries, Cottage Cheese, and Nuts
                (see one-block snack chart, page 159)
Dinner . . . . . . .Marinated Steak Kebab, page 93
Snack . . . . .Balanced Brownies, page 157

MONDAY

Breakfast . . . . . .Breakfast Pita, page 44
Lunch . . . . .BLT and Cheese Sandwich, page 58
Snack . . . . .Homemade 40-30-30 Bar, page 158
Dinner . . . . . . .Pork Tenderloin with Garlic
                and Mushrooms, page 101
Snack . . . . .Blueberry Muffins, page 155

TUESDAY

Breakfast . . . . . .Bagel, Cream Cheese, and Lox, page 67
Lunch . . . . .Balsamic Yogurt Salad, page 82
Snack . . . . .Crackers, String Cheese, and Nuts
                (see one-block snack chart, page 159)
Dinner . . . . . . .Balanced Tandoori Chicken, page 109
Snack . . . . .Balanced Brownies, page 157

WEDNESDAY

Breakfast . . . . . .Perfectly Balanced Oatmeal, page 29
Lunch . . . . .Better Than Tuna Sandwich, page 62
Snack . . . . .Bagel, Lox, and Avocado (see one-block
                snack chart, page 159)
Dinner . . . . . . .Linguine with Scallops and
                Red Bell Peppers, page 126
Snack . . . . .Almond Sugar Cookies, page 144

THURSDAY

Breakfast . . . . . .Tofu Scramble, page 47
Lunch . . . . .Balanced Minestrone Soup, page 87
Snack . . . . .Apple, String Cheese, and Nuts
               (see one-block snack chart, page 159)
Dinner . . . . .Baked Salmon with Tomatoes, Olives, and
               Fresh Herbs, page 121
Snack . . . . .Blueberry Muffins, page 155

FRIDAY

Breakfast . . . . . .Perfectly Balanced Oatmeal, page 29
Lunch . . . . .Chicken and Cucumber Chatt, page 72
Snack . . . . .Homemade 40-30-30 Bar, page 158
Dinner . . . . .Scallop-Vegetable Stir-Fry with an Oyster
               Sauce, page 128
Snack . . . . .Almond Sugar Cookies, page 144

SATURDAY

Breakfast . . . . . .Raisin and Spiced Apple Crepes, page 54
Lunch . . . . .Egg Salad Sandwich, page 61
Snack . . . . .Melon and Lox, page 142
Dinner . . . . .Pork Scaloppine, page 102
Snack . . . . .Homemade 40-30-30 Bar, page 158

BREAKFAST

I never used to bother with breakfast. I was out the door with a cup of coffee and if I got hungry in the morning, a donut or sweet roll was all I needed to see me through to lunch. After some time on a balanced meal plan, I found I really wanted a good breakfast. Always eat at least an hour after waking and eat frequently during the day. Don't go more than 5 hours between meals, except of course after your snack at night.

For me the simplest breakfast is fresh fruit with a couple of protein and fat blocks. In this section I've included lots of egg and meat dishes for more hearty appetites. When an egg substitute can be used instead of the real thing, use it. One quarter of a cup of egg substitute is only one block. I've checked out the several different brands, and they all seem pretty much the same to me, but if you have a favorite, use it.

Most recipes can be doubled and even tripled to serve two or more people. Do not increase the salt or other seasonings when increasing the recipe quantities. Use the seasoning called for, taste, and then add what you need. You will notice that I usually do not indicate a specific measure for salt and pepper, as you should use the amount that tastes right to you.

Cook everything on medium to low heat, and use good non-stick pans. Buy ripe, fresh fruits and vegetables. Try to stick with items that are in season. Save leftovers for lunch or as part of a snack.

You should eat oatmeal at least three times a week because of the gamma linolenic acid content. I suggest getting good, steel-cut oats from a natural foods store. I cook mine on low heat for 20 to 25 minutes, using 3 parts water to 1 part oats. If you haven't tried steel-cut oats, you're in for a real treat.

PERFECTLY BALANCED OATMEAL

One serving

A great way to start the day. This isn't your Mother's oatmeal, at least not mine. Add a little cinnamon for an extra taste treat.

1/4 steel-cut oats
1 1/4 cups water
1/8 teaspoon salt

1/2 cup 2% milk
1 tablespoon protein powder
2 teaspoons brown sugar
1 teaspoon butter

▶ Add the oats, water, and salt to a saucepan and cook over a low heat for 25 to 30 minutes, stirring constantly. Remove the oats from the heat and pour into a bowl. Add the milk, protein powder, sugar, and butter as a topping. Stir before serving.

BLOCKS PER SERVING:	
CARBS:	4
PROTEIN:	3
FAT:	3 1/2

BILL'S FAST BREAKFAST

One serving

Let's start off with recipes for people who need to get up and go. These dishes are quickly made, yet balanced. When I first started eating balanced meals, I had this every morning for two months. Make sure you pick out good ripe melons.

$^1/_2$ **cup low-fat cottage cheese**
$^1/_2$ **teaspoon ground cinnamon**
$^1/_8$ **teaspoon ground nutmeg**
$^1/_2$ **cantaloupe (or $^1/_4$ honeydew)**
3 pecans, chopped

▶ Put the cottage cheese in a bowl and blend in the cinnamon and nutmeg. Dice the cantaloupe and mix it with the cottage cheese. Sprinkle the nuts over the top.

BLOCKS PER SERVING:	
CARBS:	2
PROTEIN:	2
FAT:	2

YOGURT FOR BREAKFAST

Two servings

You can change your quick morning meals now and then by substituting flavored yogurt for plain. Strawberry or lemon goes well with the mint and fruit cocktail.

> **1 cup low-fat yogurt**
> **2 tablespoons vanilla protein powder**
> **$1/2$ teaspoon dried mint**
> **1 cup fruit cocktail, drained**
> **4 teaspoons slivered almonds**

▶ In a serving bowl, mix the yogurt with the protein powder and mint flakes. Stir in the fruit cocktail and top with the almonds.

Half of this recipe equals 1 serving.

BLOCKS PER SERVING:	
CARBS:	2
PROTEIN:	2
FAT:	2

COTTAGE CHEESE AND MIXED FRUIT

Two servings

For a different taste, try substituting fresh chopped mint leaves for the parsley. If you prefer honeydew melon to cantaloupe, use half the amount.

1 cup low-fat cottage cheese
1/2 teaspoon minced fresh parsley
1/8 teaspoon ground nutmeg
1/2 cantaloupe, cubed
1 cup sliced strawberries
1/2 cup grapes
2 teaspoons chopped pecans

▶ In a serving bowl, mix the cottage cheese with the parsley and nutmeg. Add the cantaloupe, strawberries, and grapes. Top with the pecans.

Half of this recipe equals 1 serving.

BLOCKS PER SERVING:	
CARBS:	2
PROTEIN:	2
FAT:	2

ALL-AMERICAN CHEESE OMELET

Two servings

This recipe is a great way to start the day, especially for those of you who eat 4-block meals. Don't make my mistake of using a low- or non-fat cheddar cheese. It cooks into a rubbery mess. Use the real thing. When seasoning this and the other omelets with cheese, don't forget that cheese by nature is salty.

1¼ teaspoons canola oil
1 egg
2 egg whites
1 teaspoon fresh parsley, chopped
⅛ teaspoon nutmeg
Salt and pepper
⅛ cup cheddar cheese, grated
½ cup chopped tomato

▶ In a nonstick omelet pan heat the oil over medium heat. Whip together the egg, egg whites, parsley, nutmeg, salt, and pepper. Add the egg mixture to the heated pan and cook for 2 minutes. Loosen the edges of the omelet and flip it over, cook until set. Sprinkle the cheese evenly down the center and fold the omelet in half. Continue cooking for 1 or 2 minutes, or until the omelet is cooked through and the cheese has melted.

▶ Top with the chopped tomato and serve. Make up the missing carbohydrate by serving 1 piece of toast or 1 whole wheat English muffin, or 1 cup sliced strawberries.

Half of this recipe equals 1 serving.

BLOCKS PER SERVING:	
CARBS:	½
PROTEIN:	2
FAT:	2

HUEVOS RANCHEROS OMELET

Two servings

1 cup salsa (see page 14)
1¼ rounded teaspoons canola oil
1 egg
2 egg whites
⅛ teaspoon chili powder
Salt and pepper
3 tablespoons Monterey Jack cheese, grated
3 tablespoons cheddar cheese, grated
2 teaspoons chopped, fresh cilantro

▶ In a small saucepan over a moderate heat, warm the salsa until heated through. Keep warm.

▶ Heat the oil in a nonstick pan over medium heat. Mix together the egg, egg whites, chili powder, salt, and pepper. Cook the eggs for 1 minute. Loosen the sides of the omelet and turn it over. Sprinkle both cheeses down the center of the omelet, cover, and cook for 1 minute, until the omelet is set and the cheese has melted.

▶ Remove from the heat and transfer to a serving plate. Spoon the salsa down the center of the omelet and fold it over. Garnish with the chopped cilantro. Make up the missing carbohydrate block with ½ cantaloupe.

Half of this recipe equals 1 serving.

BLOCKS PER SERVING:	
CARBS:	1
PROTEIN:	2
FAT:	2

COTTAGE CHEESE OMELET

One serving

Try this zesty, south-of-the-border omelet. Increasing the pepper flakes will make a spicier dish, while the avocado mellows the heat a bit.

Cooking spray
$1/4$ cup egg substitute
2 egg whites
$1/4$ teaspoon dried thyme
Pinch red pepper flakes
$1/4$ cup low-fat cottage cheese
$1^1/2$ tablespoons mashed avocado
$1/8$ teaspoon lemon juice
$1/8$ teaspoon cayenne
$1/4$ cup salsa (see page 14)

▶ Coat a nonstick pan with the cooking spray. In a small bowl, mix together the egg substitute, egg whites, thyme, and pepper flakes. Add to the heated skillet and cook until the eggs have set and have been turned once. Add the cottage cheese and fold in half. Lower the heat and continue cooking to melt the cheese.

▶ In a small bowl, combine the avocado, lemon juice, and cayenne. Mix well, and spread over the omelet. Top with the salsa. Make up carbohydrate blocks with $1/2$ cantaloupe.

BLOCKS PER SERVING:	
CARBS:	1
PROTEIN:	3
FAT:	3

PROSCIUTTO-CHEESE OMELET

Two servings

The combination of the prosciutto and basil is wonderful and makes this omelet special. You can use more basil if you wish.

¹/₂ ounce prosciutto, chopped
2 tablespoons or more chopped fresh basil
2 tablespoons low-fat ricotta cheese
3 eggs, beaten
1 tablespoons water
Salt and pepper
1 teaspoon butter
2 teaspoons grated Parmesan cheese
1 whole wheat English muffin, toasted
Paprika

▶ Preheat the broiler.

▶ In a bowl, combine the prosciutto, basil, and ricotta and mix well. In another bowl, blend the eggs, water, salt and pepper. Melt the butter in a nonstick skillet, over medium heat. Add the egg mixture and cook until the bottom of the omelet is set and lightly browned. Spoon the prosciutto mixture over half the omelet. Using a spatula, fold the omelet in half, and slide onto a flameproof plate. Sprinkle the top with the Parmesan cheese and broil until the cheese is melted, about 2 minutes.

▶ Divide the omelet in two and place on the English muffin halves. Garnish with paprika.

Half of the English muffin with the omelet equals 1 serving.

BLOCKS PER SERVING:	
CARBS:	4
PROTEIN:	4
FAT:	4

ITALIAN OMELET

Two servings

This makes a great late Sunday morning breakfast. If you have friends staying over, double the recipe and buy a big Sunday paper.

1 teaspoon olive oil
1⅓ cups sliced zucchini
1½ cups sliced mushrooms
¾ cup diced onions
¾ cups tomato purée
4 egg whites
1 egg
¼ teaspoon dried oregano
¼ teaspoon dried basil
⅛ teaspoon dried marjoram
Salt and pepper
Cooking spray
1 ounce low-fat mozzarella, shredded

▶ Heat the oil in a skillet over medium heat. Add the zucchini, mushrooms, and onions. Cook, and stir for about 8 minutes or until all the liquid has cooked off. Add the tomato purée and cook for several more minutes.

▶ Mix the egg whites, egg, oregano, basil, marjoram, and salt and pepper. Using half of the ingredients, cook one omelet at a time. Add cooking spray to a nonstick pan and heat. Add half the egg mixture and cook until firm. Top with the zucchini mixture, sprinkle on the cheese, and fold the omelet over. Slide onto a plate and serve. Repeat the process.

Half of this omelet equals 1 serving.

BLOCKS PER SERVING:	
CARBS:	2
PROTEIN:	2
FAT:	2

SCRAMBLED EGGS AND BACON

Two servings

Here is a classic breakfast dish with herbs added for a different taste and look.

1½ scant tablespoons olive oil
2 ounces chopped Canadian bacon
2 teaspoons minced scallion
¾ cup egg substitute
Salt and pepper
¼ teaspoon dried dill
1 whole wheat English muffin, toasted
1 cup cubed cantaloupe

▶ In a small skillet add oil and warm over medium heat. Add the bacon and cook until heated through, about 2 minutes. Add the scallion and cook for another 30 seconds.

▶ Combine the egg substitute, salt and pepper, and dill. Add to the bacon mixture and scramble until the eggs are cooked to the desired consistency, about 2 to 3 minutes. Remove from the heat and serve with the English muffin and cantaloupe on the side.

Half of the English muffin with the scrambled egg equals 1 serving.

BLOCKS PER SERVING:	
CARBS:	2½
PROTEIN:	2½
FAT:	2½

MEDITERRANEAN SCRAMBLED EGGS

One serving

The vegetables and olives add color and texture to this well-flavored dish.

Cooking spray
1 green bell pepper, diced
$\frac{1}{3}$ cup chopped scallion
1 tablespoon chopped fresh basil
$\frac{1}{4}$ teaspoon dried oregano
$\frac{1}{8}$ teaspoon ground nutmeg
6 black olives, chopped
1 cup seeded and chopped tomatoes
$\frac{1}{2}$ cup egg substitute

▶ Coat a small skillet lightly with cooking spray and warm over medium heat. Add the bell pepper and cook until soft, about 3 minutes. Stir in the scallion, basil, oregano, nutmeg, olives, and tomatoes. Cook for 1 minute, or until the mixture is heated through. Remove from the heat and keep warm.

▶ Coat another small skillet with cooking spray and heat over medium heat. Scramble the egg substitute until cooked through, about 2 minutes. Mix with the tomato mixture.

BLOCKS PER SERVING:	
CARBS:	2
PROTEIN:	2
FAT:	2

HEARTY SCRAMBLED EGGS WITH SAUSAGE AND THYME

―――――――――――― ❧ ――――――――――――

One serving

The cream cheese gives this dish a smooth and velvety texture.

½ cup egg substitute
1 teaspoon coarse-grained mustard
Salt and pepper
Cooking spray
3 ounces cooked turkey sausage
  (like kielbasa), sliced thin and quartered
1 scallion, chopped
½ teaspoon dried thyme
1 teaspoon butter
2 teaspoons Neufchatel cheese,
  cut into pieces

► Combine the egg substitute, mustard, salt and pepper in a bowl, mix well, and set aside.

► Coat a small skillet lightly with the cooking spray and brown the sausage for about 3 minutes over medium heat. Add the scallion and thyme and cook for 2 minutes. Transfer to a bowl.

► In the same skillet, melt the butter over medium heat. Add the egg substitute and cheese, stir until the eggs are softly set and the cheese begins to melt, about 2 minutes. Add the sausage and stir until the eggs have set, about 1 minute. Make up the missing carbohydrate blocks by serving a toasted English muffin and 1 cup cubed pineapple on the side.

BLOCKS PER SERVING:	
CARBS:	TRACE
PROTEIN:	5
FAT	5

EGG MUFFIN

One serving

Here is a great breakfast to eat on the run. You can just wrap it up and take it with you. Or trying serving it as a snack.

2 eggs
¼ cup 1% milk
Pepper
4 sun-dried tomatoes
   (dry packed), chopped
2 slices Canadian bacon
1 whole wheat English muffin, toasted
¼ cup shredded lettuce

▶ In a glass bowl, combine the eggs, milk, and pepper. Beat with a fork or wire whisk until mixed. Stir in the tomatoes. Microwave on High for two minutes, stirring twice while cooking. Add the bacon to the microwave on its own plate, and microwave everything for one minute longer. Top each muffin half with half the lettuce, one piece of bacon, and half the egg mixture.

BLOCKS PER SERVING:	
CARBS:	2
PROTEIN:	2
FAT:	1

EGG AND SAUSAGE MUFFIN

Two servings

This is my favorite breakfast. I cook the sausages ahead of time and then heat them up in the microwave. This way I'm out the door quickly in the morning.

4 turkey sausages, cut in half
Cooking spray
2 eggs
2 tablespoons chopped fresh basil
Salt and pepper
1 tablespoon mashed avocado
1 whole wheat English muffin, toasted

▶ Brown the sausage on both sides in a skillet, about 4 to 5 minutes per side.

▶ Lightly coat a small skillet with cooking spray. Scramble the eggs over medium heat, adding the fresh basil, salt and pepper. Cook about 2 minutes and remove from the heat. Divide the mashed avocado between English muffin halves and spread it evenly. Top with half the sausage and half the scrambled egg.

One half English muffin equals 1 serving.

BLOCKS PER SERVING:	
CARBS:	2
PROTEIN:	2
FAT:	2

BREAKFAST QUESADILLA

Four servings

The combination of black beans and Monterey Jack cheese makes this a special treat.

4 corn tortillas
1 cup canned black beans, drained
$\frac{1}{4}$ teaspoon dried oregano
$\frac{1}{4}$ teaspoon garlic powder
$\frac{1}{8}$ teaspoon cayenne
2 teaspoons catsup
Cooking spray
4 eggs
$\frac{1}{2}$ cup Monterey Jack cheese
4 tablespoons mashed avocado

▶ Wrap the tortillas in a damp towel and microwave on High for 2 minutes. Set aside and keep warm.

▶ In a small saucepan heat the black beans, oregano, garlic powder, pepper, and catsup over moderate heat until warmed through. In a small skillet coated with cooking spray, fry the eggs over medium heat. When almost done, place $\frac{1}{4}$ of the cheese over each egg, cover, and cook until the cheese starts to melt.

▶ Put $\frac{1}{4}$ cup of the bean mixture in the center of each tortilla, cover with one fried egg and 1 tablespoon of the mashed avocado. Fold $\frac{1}{4}$ of the tortilla up, then roll against the fold to seal the bottom. Microwave the quesadillas in the damp towel for one minute longer, and serve.

One quesadilla equals 1 serving.

BLOCKS PER SERVING:	
CARBS:	2
PROTEIN:	2
FAT:	2

BREAKFAST PITA

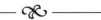

Two servings

This easy-to-make egg sandwich will leave you time to sit down and enjoy breakfast before dashing out of the house.

> 1 scant teaspoon butter
> 2 eggs
> $1/4$ teaspoon dried oregano
> Salt and pepper
> 1 pita bread, cut in half
> 2 ounces grated cheddar
> 2 tablespoons chopped fresh cilantro
> Paprika

▶ In a small saucepan, melt the butter over moderate heat. Scramble the eggs, adding the oregano, salt and pepper. Divide the eggs between the two pita halves and top with the grated cheese, cilantro, and paprika.

Half a pita equals 1 serving.

BLOCKS PER SERVING:	
CARBS:	2
PROTEIN:	2
FAT:	2

SOUTH-OF-THE-BORDER SCRAMBLE

One serving

Use spicy salsa with this scramble. As I eat more than two blocks for breakfast, I add some Canadian bacon, toast, and butter to finish off my meal.

Cooking spray
1 clove garlic, minced
3 cups sliced mushrooms
1 red bell pepper, diced
¼ teaspoon ground cumin
Salt and pepper
2 eggs, beaten
⅓ cup salsa, warmed (page 14)

▶ Lightly coat a small skillet with the cooking spray and warm over medium heat. Add the garlic and sauté until soft, about 1 minute. Stir in the mushrooms and red pepper, and cook until the pepper is soft, about 3 minutes. Add the cumin, salt and pepper. Pour in the eggs and cook until scrambled, about 2 minutes. Top with the salsa and serve.

BLOCKS PER SERVING:	
CARBS:	2
PROTEIN:	2
FAT:	2

MUSHROOM SCRAMBLE

One serving

Make this dish special by using crimini or portabello mushrooms, or a combination of several different kinds. I especially like porcini mushrooms with this recipe.

½ cup crumbled tofu
1 teaspoon canola oil
1 clove garlic, minced
2 cups sliced mushrooms
¼ cup chopped scallion
1 teaspoon minced fresh rosemary
¼ cup egg substitute
2 tablespoons shredded fontina cheese
Salt and pepper

▶ Heat the oil in a skillet over medium-high heat. Add the tofu and cook, stirring until it is golden brown. Add the garlic and cook for 1 minute. Reduce the heat to medium. Stir in the mushrooms and cook until they begin to brown. Add the scallion and rosemary. Cook for 3 to 4 minutes. Add the egg substitute and cook until it begins to set. Turn off the heat. Add the cheese, salt and pepper. Cover the skillet until the cheese just begins to melt. Transfer to a plate.

BLOCKS PER SERVING:	
CARBS:	3
PROTEIN:	3
FAT:	3

TOFU SCRAMBLE

One serving

For those who prefer to stay away from eggs, tofu makes a terrific substitute. I eat eggs but find this dish a pleasant change of pace. This recipe can be doubled for more blocks or to serve two or more people.

$1/2$ teaspoon olive oil
1 garlic clove, minced
3 cups sliced mushrooms
1 red bell pepper, seeded and chopped
$1/3$ cup chopped scallions
Salt and pepper
$1/2$ teaspoon dried thyme
$2/3$ cup cubed tofu

▶ Heat the oil in a small skillet over medium heat. Add the garlic and sauté for 2 minutes until just soft. Add the mushrooms and cook for 3 minutes. Stir in the red pepper and cook until it is soft, about 3 to 4 minutes. Add the scallions and cook for 2 minutes longer. Salt and pepper to taste and mix in the thyme. Add the tofu cubes and cook until the tofu is heated through, about 2 minutes. Serve hot.

BLOCKS PER SERVING:	
CARBS:	2
PROTEIN:	2
FAT:	2

TOFU SCRAMBLE FLORENTINE

One serving

This breakfast dish can also be served at lunch or dinner.

$\frac{1}{3}$ **cup low-sodium soy sauce**
1 clove garlic, minced
$\frac{1}{8}$ **teaspoon ground ginger**
$\frac{2}{3}$ **cup cubed tofu**
$\frac{1}{2}$ **teaspoon olive oil**
1 clove garlic, minced
$\frac{2}{3}$ **cup diced onion**
$\frac{1}{4}$ **teaspoon dried oregano**
$\frac{1}{4}$ **teaspoon dried basil**
1$\frac{1}{3}$ cups chopped fresh spinach
$\frac{1}{2}$ **teaspoon dry roasted sesame seeds**

▶ In a bowl, combine the soy sauce, garlic, and ginger. Add the tofu and marinate for at least two hours.

▶ Heat the oil in a small skillet over medium heat. Add the garlic and sauté until it is soft, about 1 minute. Add the onion, and cook it until it starts to sweat. Stir in the oregano, basil, and spinach. Cook until the spinach has wilted. Drain the tofu, and add it to the spinach mixture. Discard the marinade. Cook until the tofu is heated through. Transfer to a plate, sprinkle the sesame seeds over the top, and serve warm.

BLOCKS PER SERVING:	
CARBS:	2
PROTEIN:	2
FAT:	2

CRUSTLESS CLASSIC QUICHE

——————— ⌘ ———————

Four servings

If any of this classic dish is left over, it's a great cold snack.

2 eggs, lightly beaten
1 cup 2% milk
1/2 teaspoon salt
2 tablespoons sour cream
1/4 teaspoon ground nutmeg
1 teaspoon olive oil
12 cups chopped spinach
3 cups sliced mushrooms
6 teaspoons imitation bacon bits
Cooking spray
Heaping 1/2 cup non-fat Swiss cheese, grated

▶ Preheat the oven to 350° F.

▶ In a large glass mixing cup, combine the eggs, milk, salt, sour cream, and nutmeg. Blend with a fork or a wire whisk until smooth and creamy. Set aside.

▶ Heat the oil in a skillet over medium heat and add the spinach and mushrooms. Sauté until the spinach has wilted and the mushrooms are soft, about 4 minutes. Stir in the bacon bits.

▶ Lightly coat the bottom of a glass pie plate with cooking spray and spread the spinach mixture evenly over the bottom of the plate. Sprinkle on the cheese and pour the custard over the top. Jiggle the plate a bit to help the custard settle.

▶ Bake for about 40 minutes, or until the quiche is golden and firm. Turn the oven off and continue cooking for another 10 minutes to finish up. Cut into eight wedges and serve.

Two wedges equals 1 serving.

BLOCKS PER SERVING:	
CARBS:	1+
PROTEIN:	2
FAT:	2

CRUSTLESS VEGETABLE AND ALMOND QUICHE

Four servings

2 eggs, lightly beaten
1 cup 2% milk
$\frac{1}{2}$ teaspoon salt
1 teaspoon olive oil
1 cup diced onion
1 clove garlic, minced
$\frac{1}{4}$ teaspoon dried basil
Cooking spray
Heaping $\frac{1}{2}$ cup cheddar cheese, grated
   (Don't use non-fat or low-fat cheese)
5 teaspoons slivered almonds
1 cup cooked peas
Pepper

▶ Preheat the oven to 350° F.

▶ In a large mixing cup, combine the eggs, milk, and salt. Mix well with a fork or a wire whisk. Heat the oil in a small skillet over medium heat and add the onion and garlic. Sauté until the onions are soft. Mix in the basil and remove from the heat.

▶ Lightly coat a glass pie plate with cooking spray.

▶ This quiche is made in three layers. Start with the onion mixture and spread it evenly over the pie plate. Then sprinkle on the onions, cheese, almonds, and peas. Pour the custard over the top and jiggle the plate a bit to help everything settle. Season with the pepper.

▶ Bake for 40 minutes, or until the top is golden and firm. Turn the oven off and leave the quiche in another 10 minutes to finish cooking. Cut into eight wedges and serve. Make up the missing carbohydrate blocks with $\frac{1}{2}$ slice toasted whole wheat bread.

Two wedges equal 1 serving.

BLOCKS PER SERVING:	
CARBS:	$1\frac{1}{3}$
PROTEIN:	2
FAT:	2

FRENCH TOAST AND BACON

Two servings

Cooking spray
3 ounces Canadian bacon
$\frac{1}{2}$ cup egg substitute
1 tablespoon 1% milk
$\frac{1}{4}$ teaspoon ground cinnamon
$\frac{1}{8}$ teaspoon ground nutmeg
Pinch salt
2 slices whole wheat bread
$\frac{1}{2}$ teaspoon powdered sugar
1 cup sliced strawberries

▶ Lightly coat a small skillet with cooking spray and heat the pan over medium heat. Add the bacon and cook until heated through, about 1 minute on each side. Remove from the heat, set aside, and keep warm.

▶ Mix together the egg substitute, milk, cinnamon, nutmeg, and salt, and pour onto a plate. Soak the bread in the mixture for 1 or 2 seconds on each side until well coated. Heat another skillet coated with cooking spray over medium heat. Add the bread and cook for 2 or 3 minutes on each side, or until it is golden brown and heated through. Remove the cooked bread to a plate, dust with the powdered sugar, top with the strawberries, and serve with the bacon.

▶ If you prefer, you can omit the powdered sugar and strawberries, and top each slice of French toast with $1\frac{1}{2}$ teaspoons maple syrup.

One slice of french toast equals 1 serving.

BLOCKS PER SERVING:	
CARBS:	$2\frac{1}{2}$
PROTEIN:	$2\frac{1}{2}$
FAT:	1

CREPES

Sixteen servings

The Basic Crepe

I love to make crepes. They are easy and such fun. Double or triple the recipe and make up a bunch ahead of time.

3 eggs
1 cup flour
⅔ cup 2% milk
¾ cup soda water
2 tablespoons canola oil
Pinch salt
Cooking spray

▶ Combine all the ingredients, except the cooking spray, in a blender or food processor. Process until the batter is smooth, stopping once or twice to scrape down the sides of the container with a rubber spatula.

▶ Cover and refrigerate the batter for at least 1 hour.
Lightly coat a 6-inch crepe pan with cooking spray and warm over moderate heat. Stir the batter well and pour just enough into the pan to make a thin coating. Cook each crepe until set, about 1 minute. Turn and cook the other side about 1 minute. Transfer to a sheet of parchment or waxed paper. Do not stack the crepes until they are completely cool.

▶ When they are cool, put wax paper between them. If you are refrigerating them, simply put them in a plastic bag, secured with a tie. If you are freezing them, wrap the plastic bag in aluminum foil, as an extra measure of protection.

▶ Completely cooled crepes can be stacked, wrapped in aluminum foil, and refrigerated for up to five days or frozen for up to two months. Thaw in a warm oven.

BLOCKS PER SERVING:	
CARBS:	½
PROTEIN:	TRACE
FAT:	1

STRAWBERRIES AND CREPES

Two servings

Use big ripe berries for this recipe. If you wish, other kinds of berries or melon slices, can be used instead.

2 cups fresh sliced strawberries
¹/₂ teaspoon orange extract
¹/₂ tablespoon sour cream
¹/₂ cup yogurt
2 tablespoons protein powder
¹/₂ teaspoon sugar
4 basic crepes (page 52)
Pinch of ground cinnamon

▶ Pick out firm strawberries and slice them thin. Sprinkle on the orange extract and set aside. In a small bowl, combine the sour cream, yogurt, protein powder, and sugar. Mix until smooth and creamy.

▶ Prepare the basic crepe recipe.

▶ Divide the strawberries among the four crepes and roll them up. Top with the sour cream mixture and garnish with the cinnamon.

Two crepes equals 1 serving.

BLOCKS PER SERVING:	
CARBS:	5
PROTEIN:	5
FAT:	5

RAISIN AND SPICED APPLE CREPES

Four servings

These crepes, with their chewy, spicy filling, make a perfect morning starter.

> **1 cup peeled, cored, and diced apples**
> **$1/2$ teaspoon ground cinnamon**
> **$1/4$ teaspoon ground nutmeg**
> **$1/8$ teaspoon ground allspice**
> **2 teaspoons ground walnuts**
> **5 tablespoons golden raisins**
> **2 cups low-fat cottage cheese**
> **4 basic crepes (page 52)**
> **1 teaspoon butter**

▶ In a bowl, combine the apples, cinnamon, nutmeg, allspice, and ground walnuts. Mix in the raisins and cottage cheese and set aside.

▶ Prepare the crepe recipe.

▶ Divide the apple mixture among the four crepes and roll each one up, tucking in both ends of the crepe as it is rolled to form a seal.

▶ Melt half of the butter in a small skillet over moderate heat and add two crepes. Cook for 2 minutes, reduce the heat, turn the crepes over, and cook for 2 minutes longer. Repeat with the remaining butter and crepes.

One crepe equals 1 serving.

BLOCKS PER SERVING:	
CARBS:	2
PROTEIN:	2
FAT:	2

BLINTZES WITH BLUEBERRIES

Four servings

These Russian-style crepes are filled with sweetened cottage and yogurt cheese. I've jazzed them up a bit to balance them. They are good for breakfast, lunch, or dinner.

1 cup low-fat yogurt
4 basic crepes (page 52)
1¼ cups low-fat cottage cheese
2 tablespoons protein powder
2 teaspoons lemon zest
2 tablespoons fresh lemon juice
½ teaspoon ground cinnamon
4 teaspoons sugar
2 and 1 scant ½ teaspoons butter
2½ cups fresh blueberries

▶ Drain the yogurt to make yogurt cheese (page 15).

▶ Prepare the Basic Crepe recipe.

▶ In a bowl, combine the yogurt cheese, cottage cheese, protein powder, lemon zest, lemon juice, cinnamon, and sugar. Mix until smooth and creamy.

▶ Distribute the mixture over the four crepes and roll them up. While rolling up each crepe tuck in both ends to make a seal.

▶ Melt half the butter in a small skillet over moderate heat and add two crepes. Cook for 2 minutes until lightly browned. Lower the heat and carefully turn the blintzes over and cook for 2 more minutes. Repeat with the remaining butter and crepes. Transfer the blintzes to serving plates. Sprinkle the berries over the top as a garnish.

One crepe equals 1 serving.

BLOCKS PER SERVING:	
CARBS:	3
PROTEIN:	3
FAT:	3

LUNCH

Many of us take lunch along with us to work. I have included a good number of recipes for sandwiches and sandwich-type combinations, and for items that travel well in a container. Load up on lots of "free foods," like sprouts and iceberg lettuce with your lunch. Most recipes in this section can be prepared ahead of time, wrapped or sealed tightly, and used when needed.

For those recipes with spreads, dressings, or sauces, I usually make up extra amounts. This serves two purposes. First I have a good supply, and second it's easier for me to work in bigger quantities. Sealed tightly, most spreads last for weeks chilled. A good rule of thumb for a spread or dressing is: $\frac{1}{4}$ rounded teaspoon equals about one block fat.

Here are some ideas for lunch: several Lean Cuisine entrées are four blocks and are balanced for the most part. You need to read the labels. Also several Progresso soups are balanced. Each can be about four blocks. My favorite is Beef Barley.

CHICKEN SALAD SANDWICH

Two servings

Deli-style chicken meat works best in this great balanced open-faced sandwich. I prefer light canola mayonnaise to regular mayonnaise on my sandwiches. I like the flavor better.

4$^{1}/_{2}$ ounces chicken meat, shredded and chopped
1 celery rib, chopped
$^{1}/_{8}$ chopped onion
2 tablespoons light canola mayonnaise
Salt and pepper
$^{1}/_{4}$ teaspoon dried dill
$^{1}/_{8}$ teaspoon hot paprika
4 teaspoons dill pickle relish
2 slices whole wheat bread
4 tomato slices
$^{1}/_{4}$ cup shredded lettuce
3 tablespoons low-fat Monterey Jack cheese, shredded

▶ In a bowl, combine the chicken, celery, onion, mayonnaise, salt, and pepper, dill, paprika, and pickle relish. Mix well. Divide and spread the chicken mixture evenly on the bread. Top with the tomato, lettuce, and cheese.

One slice of bread with topping
equals 1 serving.

BLOCKS PER SERVING:	
CARBS:	2$^{1}/_{2}$
PROTEIN:	2$^{1}/_{2}$
FAT:	2$^{1}/_{2}$

BLT AND CHEESE SANDWICH

Two servings

I enjoy eating balanced meals now. The best part is that they are made up mostly of food I was eating anyway. I've just changed the proportions.

Cooking spray
3 ounces Canadian bacon
2 tablespoons light canola mayonnaise
2 teaspoons sweet pickle relish
Salt and pepper
1 teaspoon chopped fresh parsley
2 slices whole wheat bread, toasted
$\frac{1}{4}$ cup grated cheddar cheese
$\frac{1}{2}$ cup shredded lettuce
4 slices tomato

▶ Lightly coat a small skillet with cooking spray and warm over medium heat. Cook the bacon until heated through, about 2 minutes on each side. In a small bowl, combine the mayonnaise, relish, salt and pepper, and parsley, mix well, and spread over the two pieces of bread. Top with the bacon, cheddar cheese, lettuce, and tomato.

One piece of bread with topping equals 1 serving.

BLOCKS PER SERVING:	
CARBS:	$2\frac{1}{2}$
PROTEIN:	$2\frac{1}{2}$
FAT:	$2\frac{1}{2}$

TURKEY AND BACON SANDWICH

Two servings

Turkey and bacon taste very good together on this open-faced sandwich.

> 2 tablespoons light canola mayonnaise
> $1/2$ teaspoon paprika
> $1/8$ teaspoon pepper
> 2 slices whole wheat bread
> 1 ounce Canadian bacon, cooked and drained
> 5 ounces sliced deli-style turkey meat
> 1 tomato, sliced
> $1/2$ cup alfalfa sprouts
> 2 pickle slices

▶ In a small bowl, combine the mayonnaise, paprika, and pepper. Mix well. Divide and spread evenly over the two slices of bread. Top with the bacon, turkey, tomato slices, sprouts, and pickle.

One slice of bread with topping equals 1 serving.

BLOCKS PER SERVING:	
CARBS:	$2^1/2$
PROTEIN:	$2^1/2$
FAT:	$2^1/2$

GRILLED CHICKEN AND CHEESE SANDWICH

Two servings

For a change, try this tasty chicken combination with different cheeses. I use try a sharp cheddar on mine occasionally.

1½ teaspoons butter, divided
2 slices whole wheat bread
2 teaspoons Dijon-style mustard
4 ounces deli-style chicken meat, sliced thin and
    divided
Salt and pepper
2 slices tomato
3 tablespoons shredded low-fat mozzarella cheese

▶ Thinly spread the butter on one side of each bread slice then spread the mustard on the opposite side. Place in a large heavy-bottomed skillet, butter side down. Top with the chicken, salt and pepper, and one slice of tomato on each half. Sprinkle on the mozzarella cheese. Cover and cook over medium-low heat until the cheese has melted, about 3 minutes.

One slice of bread with topping
equals 1 serving.

BLOCKS PER SERVING:	
CARBS:	2½
PROTEIN:	2½
FAT:	2½

EGG SALAD SANDWICH

Two servings

For this complete sandwich, bite the bullet and use real eggs. In my experience an egg substitute just won't work here.

2 eggs, hard-boiled and cooled
2 tablespoons light canola mayonnaise
$1/2$ cup low-fat cottage cheese
1 ounce Parmesan cheese, grated
2 teaspoons minced green onion
Salt and pepper
$1/4$ teaspoon curry powder
2 slices whole wheat bread, toasted
$1/4$ cucumber, peeled and sliced thin
1 tomato, sliced
$1/2$ cup shredded lettuce
$1/4$ teaspoon paprika

▶ In a small bowl, mash the eggs with a fork. Add the mayonnaise, cottage cheese, Parmesan cheese, onion, salt and pepper, and curry. Mix well.

▶ Place half the cucumber, tomato, and lettuce on each piece of bread. Divide the egg mixture between the two and sprinkle on the paprika.

One slice of bread with topping equals 1 serving.

BLOCKS PER SERVING:	
CARBS:	$2^1/2$
PROTEIN:	$2^1/2$
FAT:	$2^1/2$

BETTER THAN TUNA SANDWICH

Two servings

Remember that most spices are free food! So experiment and use them to pick up an often ordinary recipe. Dill goes well with tuna, as does lots of fresh parsley.

1 6-ounce can tuna
2 tablespoons light canola mayonnaise
1 teaspoon Dijon-style mustard
2 teaspoons sweet relish
$1/4$ teaspoon ground celery seed
$1/8$ teaspoon ground coriander
Salt and pepper
3 tablespoons chopped fresh parsley
2 slices whole wheat bread, toasted
$1/2$ cup shredded lettuce
1 tomato, sliced thin
$1/2$ cup alfalfa sprouts

▶ In a small bowl, combine the tuna, mayonnaise, mustard, relish, celery seed, coriander, salt and pepper, and parsley. Mix well. Divide the mixture between the two slices of bread, top with the lettuce, tomato, and sprouts.

One slice of bread with topping equals 1 serving.

BLOCKS PER SERVING:	
CARBS:	$2^1/2$
PROTEIN:	$2^1/2$
FAT:	$2^1/2$

BAGEL WITH SALMON SPREAD

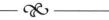

Two servings

As salmon is a good source of EPA (eicosapentaenoic acid), try to include it in your diet several times a week. Here's a zesty sandwich that does it for you.

6 ounces canned pink salmon (or 6 ounces cooked)
1 tablespoon "Philly Free" cream cheese, softened
1 tablespoon low-fat sour cream
$\frac{1}{2}$ tablespoon chopped fresh dill
1 tablespoon minced red onion
$\frac{1}{4}$ cup minced celery
3 black olives, chopped
Salt and pepper
1 bagel, cut in half
$\frac{1}{2}$ cup shredded butter lettuce
$\frac{1}{2}$ teaspoon paprika

▶ In a bowl, combine the salmon, cream cheese, sour cream, dill, onion, celery, olives, salt and pepper. Mix well. Cover and chill for 1 hour. Divide the lettuce between the two bagel halves, top with the salmon mixture, and dust with the paprika.

One half bagel with topping equals 1 serving.

BLOCKS PER SERVING:	
CARBS:	$2\frac{1}{2}$
PROTEIN:	$2\frac{1}{2}$
FAT:	$2\frac{1}{2}$

PHILLY CHEESE PIZZA BREAD

Two servings

Here's a new twist to a great classic sandwich. Using your toaster oven makes preparation of this meal very easy indeed.

1 and 1 scant ¹/₂ teaspoons olive oil, divided
¹/₂ onion, sliced thin
¹/₂ green bell pepper, julienned
¹/₄ teaspoon pepper
4¹/₂ ounces deli-style sliced roast beef
3 tablespoons grated low-fat Swiss cheese
1 whole wheat English muffin, cut in half

▶ Preheat the oven broiler, or use your toaster oven.

▶ Heat ¹/₂ the oil in a small skillet over medium heat until hot. Add the onion and sauté for 5 minutes, stirring frequently. Stir in the bell pepper and pepper, and cook until the bell pepper is tender, about 3 minutes.

▶ Drizzle the remaining oil on both halves of the muffin evenly. Top with the beef, onion mixture, and grated cheese.

▶ Place the muffins on a baking sheet lined with foil and broil 6 inches from the heat for about 2 minutes, or until the cheese melts.

One half English muffin with topping equals 1 serving.

BLOCKS PER SERVING:	
CARBS:	2¹/₂
PROTEIN:	2¹/₂
FAT:	2

SALAMI AND SUN-DRIED TOMATO PIZZA BREAD

Two servings

The roasted garlic gives this hearty-tasting sandwich a sweet buttery flavor.

1 whole wheat English muffin, cut in half
1 scant teaspoon olive oil
2 tablespoons tomato sauce
2 ounces salami
4 sun-dried tomatoes, chopped
1/4 onion, sliced thin
2 teaspoons roasted garlic (page 13)
6 black olives, chopped fine
1/4 cup shredded low-fat mozzarella cheese

▶ Preheat the toaster oven.

▶ Lay out the two halves of the English muffin on the baking sheet lined with tin foil. Drizzle the oil over the bread and let it soak in. Cover the top of each muffin with tomato sauce. Top each muffin with half the salami, tomatoes, onion, garlic, olives, and cheese. Place in the toaster oven about 6 inches from the heat and broil for 2 to 3 minutes, or until the cheese is melted and bubbly.

One half English muffin with topping equals 1 serving.

BLOCKS PER SERVING:	
CARBS:	2+
PROTEIN:	2
FAT:	2

SALMON PIZZA BREAD

Two servings

With a toaster oven, this pizza bread is a snap to make.

1 whole wheat English muffin, cut in half
1½ scant teaspoons olive oil
2 teaspoons chopped fresh dill
¼ onion, sliced thin
3 ounces smoked salmon or lox
3 tablespoons crumbled Brie cheese
1 tablespoon minced scallion (green tops only)

▶ Preheat the oven broiler, or use your toaster oven.

▶ Lay both halves of the English muffin on the toaster oven tray or a baking sheet lined with aluminum foil. Brush 2 teaspoons of oil over each half and let it soak in. Top each with half the dill, onion, salmon, and cheese. Put under the broiler, about 6 inches from the heat, for 2 to 3 minutes, or until the cheese melts. Remove from the oven, and garnish with the scallion.

One half English muffin with topping equals 1 serving.

BLOCKS PER SERVING:	
CARBS:	2
PROTEIN:	2
FAT:	2

BAGEL, CREAM CHEESE, AND LOX

Two servings

I like the combination of bagels, cream cheese, and lox so much I could hardly believe it could make a balanced meal until I checked it out. Enjoy!

3 tablespoons "Philly Free" cream cheese, softened
2 teaspoons minced scallion
1/2 clove garlic, minced
1 bagel, cut in half
3 ounces lox or smoked salmon

▶ In a small bowl combine the cream cheese, scallion, and garlic. Mix until smooth and creamy. Spread the mixture on the bagel halves. Top with the lox.

One half bagel with topping equals 1 serving.

BLOCKS PER SERVING:	
CARBS:	2
PROTEIN:	2
FAT:	2

BAGEL WITH SALMON SPREAD

One serving

This is a great topping for a bagel. One of our local bagel shops makes a similar spread and it is very popular. Here's my version.

> $^1\!/_2$ **cup non-fat yogurt**
> **1 teaspoon sugar**
> **5 ounces smoked salmon, chopped fine**
> **2$^1\!/_2$ tablespoons "Philly Free" cream cheese**
> **1 tablespoon minced scallion**
> $^1\!/_2$ **teaspoon dried dill**
> $^1\!/_2$ **bagel, toasted**
> **Pinch paprika**

▶ Drain the yogurt to make yogurt cheese (page 15). The mixture will be as thick as cream cheese, but slightly more tart. Add the sugar and mix until smooth and creamy. Stir in the salmon, scallion, and dill. Mix well. Spread over the toasted bagel half and garnish with paprika.

BLOCKS PER SERVING:	
CARBS:	4
PROTEIN:	4
FAT:	4

BLT PITA

Two servings

Here is my special twist on a old classic. Quick and easy, it makes a balanced lunch for yourself or for sharing with a friend.

> 1 tablespoon light canola mayonnaise
> 1 teaspoon Dijon-style mustard
> 2 teaspoons minced scallion
> Salt and pepper
> 1 pita bread, cut in half
> 4 ounces Canadian bacon, sliced and cooked
> 1 cup shredded lettuce
> 1 tomato, chopped

▶ In a small bowl, combine the mayonnaise, mustard, scallion, salt and pepper. Mix with a fork until smooth and creamy.

▶ Divide the bacon between the two pita bread halves, top with the lettuce and tomato. Spoon the sauce over the top.

One half a pita with topping equals 1 serving.

BLOCKS PER SERVING:	
CARBS:	2
PROTEIN:	2
FAT:	2

CHICKEN SALAD PITA

Two servings

I prefer pita sandwiches because they are easy to wrap up and take along for a lunch on the run. Try adding cucumber, celery, or sprouts for a different taste and texture.

6 ounces deli-style chicken, shredded
1 teaspoon Dijon-style mustard
4 teaspoons light canola mayonnaise
$1/2$ onion, chopped
2 tablespoons shredded carrot
Salt and pepper
1 pita bread, cut in half
1 cup shredded lettuce
1 small tomato, sliced thin

▶ In a bowl, mix the chicken, mustard, canola mayonnaise, onion, carrot, salt, and pepper. Divide the mixture between the two pita halves, top with the lettuce and tomato.

One half a pita with topping equals 1 serving.

BLOCKS PER SERVING:	
CARBS:	2
PROTEIN:	2
FAT:	2

BROILED TOFU PITA

Two servings

I always seem to be in a hurry and look for ways to save time. Having ingredients ready to use is a great help, so I make up extra tofu, keep it chilled, knowing it will last several days, covered, in the refrigerator.

¼ cup low-sodium soy sauce
1 clove garlic, minced
¼ teaspoon minced fresh ginger
½ cup cubed extra-firm tofu
1 pita bread, cut in half
3 tablespoons shredded Monterey Jack cheese
2 slices avocado, either mashed or sliced

▶ Combine the soy sauce, garlic, and ginger in a bowl. Add the tofu to marinate, cover, and chill for at least 4 hours or overnight.

▶ Preheat the broiler.

▶ Remove the tofu from the marinade. Discard the marinade. Place the tofu on a flameproof plate or pan and broil it for 3 to 4 minutes about 6 inches from the heat, turning once. Divide the tofu between the two pita halves, top with equal amounts of cheese and avocado.

One half a pita with topping equals 1 serving.

BLOCKS PER SERVING:	
CARBS:	2
PROTEIN:	2½
FAT:	2

CHICKEN AND CUCUMBER CHATT

One serving

I like putting a salad into a pita for a wonderful combination of tastes. Chatt is a spicy but cool Indian salad, and I stuff it into pita bread to make a balanced sandwich.

7 ounces deli-style chicken meat, shredded
1 teaspoon red pepper flakes
Salt and pepper
¹⁄₄ cup white wine vinegar
3 tablespoons light canola mayonnaise
¹⁄₂ teaspoon ground mustard
¹⁄₄ teaspoon ground cumin
¹⁄₃ cup chopped onion
¹⁄₂ pita bread
1 cucumber, peeled, halved lengthwise, seeded, and
**   thinly sliced**
¹⁄₄ cup chopped fresh mint

▶ In a bowl, combine the chicken, pepper flakes, salt and pepper. Mix well, and set aside.

▶ In a food processor or blender, combine the vinegar, mayonnaise, mustard seed, cumin, and onion. Process until the onion is finely minced. Transfer to a bowl, cover, and chill for 1 hour.

▶ Fill the pita with the chicken mixture, add the cucumber, pour on the sauce, and top with the mint.

BLOCKS PER SERVING:	
CARBS:	4
PROTEIN:	5
FAT:	5

MEDITERRANEAN TUNA PITA

One serving

This is a zesty variation on a traditional French salad.

4 ounces canned tuna
Salt and pepper
1 teaspoon olive oil
1 clove garlic, minced
1 tomatoes, peeled and chopped
2 scallions, white parts only, finely chopped
1 green bell pepper, seeded and chopped
1 tablespoon capers, drained
1 tablespoon chopped fresh flat leaf parsley
1 tablespoon chopped fresh mint
1 teaspoon minced fresh thyme
2 tablespoons fresh lemon juice
2 teaspoon Dijon-style mustard
¹/₂ pita bread

▶ In a bowl, combine the tuna, salt and pepper, olive oil, and garlic. Mix well and set aside.

▶ In a larger bowl, combine the tomato, green pepper, capers, parsley, mint, and thyme, and toss. Blend the lemon juice and mustard until smooth and toss with the tomato mixture.

▶ Fill the pita bread with the tuna and tomato mixture.

BLOCKS PER SERVING:	
CARBS:	4
PROTEIN:	4
FAT:	4

RED LENTIL AND PARMESAN PITA

Two servings

When I cook lentils, I always make an extra amount, because they are a favorable carbohydrate source. It's a good idea to have some on hand in the refrigerator, ready for a tasty combination like this.

1/4 cup cooked red lentils
4 ounces grated Parmesan cheese
Fresh ground pepper, to taste
1/4 teaspoon dried thyme
1/8 teaspoon ground cumin
1/2 pita bread
1 tablespoon tahini sauce (page 15)
1/4 cup alfalfa sprouts
1/2 tomato, chopped

▶ In a bowl, combine the lentils, cheese, pepper, thyme, and cumin. Mix well. Fill the pita bread with the lentil mixture, spoon on the tahini sauce, top with the sprouts and tomato.

One quarter of pita bread with topping equals 1 serving.

BLOCKS PER SERVING:	
CARBS:	2
PROTEIN:	2
FAT:	2

TOFU PITA SANDWICH

One serving

I like to combine pita bread and tofu for a balanced meal. Although tofu has a bland taste, it readily absorbs other flavors that you add to it.

¼ cup cubed firm tofu
1 scallion, chopped
3 tablespoons chopped red bell pepper
2 teaspoons light canola mayonnaise
½ teaspoon Dijon-style mustard
½ teaspoon white wine vinegar
Salt and pepper
½ pita bread
½ cup shredded butter lettuce
¼ cup chopped tomato

▶ In a bowl, combine the tofu, scallion, red pepper, mayonnaise, mustard, vinegar, salt and pepper. Let this mixture stand for 15 to 30 minutes so that the tofu will absorb the spices. Spoon the mixture into the pita half, top with the lettuce and tomato.

BLOCKS PER SERVING:	
CARBS:	2½
PROTEIN:	2
FAT:	2

TUNISIAN PITA WITH AVOCADO

Two servings

I have taken a North African salad dish—an unusual combination of flavors and textures—and turned into a balanced pita sandwich.

$^1/_2$ red bell pepper, roasted and chopped
2 tablespoons chopped red onion
$^1/_2$ apple, peeled, cored, and diced
1 tomato, diced
1 teaspoon minced jalapeño pepper
1 teaspoon fresh lemon juice
$^1/_4$ teaspoon dried mint leaves
$^1/_2$ cup crumbled feta cheese
$^1/_2$ pita bread
4 teaspoons mashed avocado

▶ Mix together all the ingredients except the pita bread and the avocado. Spoon the mixture into the pita bread, and top with the avocado.

One quarter pita bread with topping equals 1 serving.

BLOCKS PER SERVING:	
CARBS:	2
PROTEIN:	2
FAT:	2

LUNCHTIME QUESADILLA

Two servings

For any south-of-the-border recipe, be sure to use only fresh tortilla shells. I have one problem with this recipe—it's so good, I can find myself eating too many blocks if I'm not careful.

2 corn tortillas
$1/4$ cup shredded Monterey Jack cheese
$1/4$ cup shredded cheddar cheese
2 tablespoons diced onion
1 jalapeño pepper, diced
Cooking spray
$1/2$ cup salsa (page 14)
2 tablespoons guacamole (page 12)

▶ Soften the tortillas by placing them in a damp towel folded in half and microwaving them for 2 minutes. Sprinkle the cheese evenly over the tortillas. Top with the onion and the jalapeño. Roll up the tortillas and flatten.

▶ Heat a heavy-bottomed skillet coated lightly with cooking spray over medium heat. Add the quesadillas to the pan and cook about 2 minutes on each side, or until the cheese has melted. Remove to a plate. Spoon half the salsa over each quesadilla and top with half the guacamole.

One tortilla with topping
equals 1 serving.

BLOCKS PER SERVING:	
CARBS:	2
PROTEIN:	2
FAT:	2

CHICKEN FAJITAS

Two servings

For a change of pace, substitute lean pork or beef for the chicken, and you'll have two more versions of this easy-to-make dish.

Cooking spray
4 ounces boneless chicken meat, cut into thin strips
Salt and pepper
$1/8$ teaspoon ground cumin
$1/8$ teaspoon dried paprika
$1/8$ teaspoon dried oregano
$1/4$ cup water
1 onion, thinly sliced
1 green bell pepper, seeded and sliced
1 red bell pepper, seeded and sliced
$1/2$ jalapeño pepper, seeded and chopped
1 flour tortilla, cut in half
2 tablespoons guacamole (page 12)

▶ Coat a skillet lightly with cooking spray and brown the chicken over medium heat. Add the salt and pepper, cumin, paprika, oregano, and water. Mix well and cook until the water evaporates.

▶ Coat another skillet lightly with cooking spray and over medium heat sauté the onion and bell peppers until soft. Add the jalapeño pepper to the bell pepper mixture and cook for 1 minute. Give the mixture one more toss and remove from the heat.

▶ Put half the chicken mixture and half the pepper mixture on each tortilla half, top with the guacamole, and roll up.

One tortilla half with topping equals 1 serving.

BLOCKS PER SERVING:	
CARBS:	2
PROTEIN:	2
FAT:	2

TOFU FAJITAS

Two servings

Here is a great recipe using tofu which is an important source of protein for millions of people around the world.

¼ cup diced extra-firm tofu
1 tablespoon chili powder
¼ teaspoon ground cumin
Cooking spray
1 small onion, thinly sliced
1 green bell pepper, seeded and sliced
1 red bell pepper, seeded and sliced
1 jalapeño pepper, chopped
1 flour tortilla, cut in half
3 tablespoons grated Monterey Jack cheese
2 tablespoons mashed guacamole, divided (page 12)

► Put the tofu squares in a plastic bag with the chili powder and cumin. Gently toss until each piece is lightly coated with the seasonings. Spray a skillet with the cooking spray and heat over medium heat. Remove the tofu from the bag and brown on all sides in the heated skillet.

► Coat another skillet lightly with the cooking spray and heat over medium heat. Add the onion and bell peppers and cook for about 3 minutes, or until they are soft. Divide the tofu and the peppers between the two tortilla halves, sprinkle with the cheese, top with the guacamole, and roll up.

One tortilla half with topping equals 1 serving.

BLOCKS PER SERVING:	
CARBS:	2
PROTEIN:	2
FAT:	2

INDIAN CARROT AND CUCUMBER SALAD

Two servings

Here's a cooling flavorful salad for a hot day.

1 red onion, chopped
$1/4$ cup white wine vinegar
2 teaspoons sugar
1 teaspoon red pepper flakes
1 teaspoon mustard seeds
$1/4$ teaspoon ground cumin
Salt and pepper
1 carrot, shredded
2 cucumbers, peeled, seeded, and sliced thin
$1/4$ cup chopped fresh mint
$1/4$ cup chopped, dry-roasted peanuts

▶ Combine the onion, vinegar, sugar, pepper flakes, mustard seed, cumin, salt and pepper, in a blender or food processor. Process until the onion is finely minced. Taste and adjust the seasoning.

▶ In a bowl, combine the carrot and cucumber. Spoon on the onion dressing and toss. Cover and chill for at least 30 minutes.

▶ Before serving, sprinkle with the mint and peanuts. The missing protein blocks can be made up with 2 ounces of cold cuts or 2 ounces of cheese.

Half of this recipe equals 1 serving.

BLOCKS PER SERVING:	
CARBS:	$2^1/2$
PROTEIN:	0
FAT:	$2^1/2$

TOMATO WITH
CUCUMBER-MACADAMIA NUT SALAD

One serving

Plan to eat this salad as soon as it is made while the flavors are still fresh and the ingredients crisp. For a 4-carbohydrate-block sandwich, stuff half of it in a pita bread.

2 cucumbers, peeled, seeded, and shredded
1 teaspoon red pepper flakes
1 clove garlic, minced
2 tablespoon chopped fresh cilantro
2 tablespoons fresh lime juice
2 tomatoes, sliced
¹⁄₃ cup shredded low-fat mozzarella cheese
3 macadamia nuts, chopped

▶ In a large bowl, combine the cucumbers, pepper flakes, garlic, cilantro, and lime juice. Arrange the tomato slices on a plate and spoon the cucumber mixture over the top. Top with the mozzarella cheese and sprinkle on the chopped nuts.

BLOCKS PER SERVING:	
CARBS:	3
PROTEIN:	3
FAT:	3

BALSAMIC YOGURT SALAD

Two servings

This Mediterranean-style salad makes a great lunch or side dish.

1$\frac{1}{2}$ scant teaspoons olive oil
1 tablespoon balsamic vinegar
3 tablespoons low-fat yogurt
Salt and pepper
1 teaspoon dried tarragon
1 teaspoon ground coriander
2 cups chopped tomato
4 celery stalks, chopped
1 sweet onion, thinly sliced
1 green bell pepper, seeded and chopped
$\frac{1}{4}$ cup thinly sliced radishes
2 tablespoons chopped fresh parsley

▶ In a bowl, combine the oil, vinegar, yogurt, salt and pepper, tarragon, and coriander. Whisk until well mixed.

▶ Combine the tomato, celery, onion, bell pepper, and radishes in a bowl. Pour on the dressing and mix until the vegetables are evenly coated. Garnish with the parsley. The missing protein blocks can be made up with 2 ounces deli-style cold cuts or cheese, on the side.

Half of this recipe equals 1 serving.

BLOCKS PER SERVING:	
CARBS:	2
PROTEIN:	TRACE
FAT:	2

RED PEPPER SALAD WITH
TARRAGON VINAIGRETTE

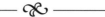

Two servings

Roasted peppers have such a special flavor. Although you can buy them commercially, try roasting them yourself. They taste better when they are homemade.

> 2 green bell peppers
> 2 red bell peppers
> 2 yellow bell peppers
> $^1/_2$ cucumber
> 3 cups chopped Romaine lettuce
> $1^1/_2$ scant teaspoons olive oil
> $1^1/_2$ scant tablespoons white wine vinegar
> 1 teaspoon Dijon-style mustard
> 2 tablespoons protein powder
> $^1/_2$ teaspoon dried tarragon
> Salt and pepper

▶ Roast the peppers (page 13) and cut into strips. Peel the cucumber. Cut it in half and remove the seeds. Julienne the two halves. Place the lettuce on a plate and arrange the cucumber and peppers on top.

▶ Put the rest of the ingredients in a food processor or blender, and blend until smooth and creamy. Pour this dressing over the pepper salad.

Half of this recipe equals 1 serving.

BLOCKS PER SERVING:	
CARBS:	2
PROTEIN:	2
FAT:	2

GREEK SALAD

Two servings

Try to get fresh oregano for this salad and use lots of it chopped up in the dressing and as topping.

> 1 teaspoon olive oil
> 1½ tablespoons lemon juice
> 2 cloves garlic, minced
> 1 teaspoon fresh oregano
> Salt and pepper
> 2 tomatoes, cubed
> 1 green bell pepper, seeded and cubed
> 1 cucumber, peeled, seeded, and cubed
> ½ cup chopped red onion
> 1 cup sliced mushrooms
> 3 Kalamata olives, chopped
> ¼ cup crumbled feta cheese
> 2 ounces salami, sliced thin and then chopped or julienned

▶ In a food processor or blender, combine the oil, lemon juice, garlic, oregano, salt and pepper. Blend until smooth and creamy.

▶ In a bowl, combine the tomatoes, bell pepper, cucumber, onion, and mushrooms. Pour the dressing over the salad and mix well. Top with the olives, cheese, salami and chopped fresh oregano, if available.

Half of this recipe equals 1 serving.

BLOCKS PER SERVING:	
CARBS:	2
PROTEIN:	2
FAT:	2

SPINACH AND FENNEL WITH TARRAGON DRESSING

––––––– ∝ℰ –––––––

Two servings

This salad offers a tasty combination of unusual ingredients. The creamy tarragon dressing given here can also serve as a topping for meat and fish.

1^1/$_2$ scant teaspoons olive oil
1 tablespoon balsamic vinegar
^{1}/$_4$ cup egg substitute
2 teaspoons Dijon-style mustard
1 teaspoon dried tarragon
Salt and pepper
^{1}/$_3$ pear, peeled and cubed
1 tablespoon lemon juice
^{1}/$_2$ cup water
4 cups fresh torn spinach leaves
1 fennel bulb, diced
1 cup thinly sliced mushrooms
3 strips bacon, cooked and crumbled

▶ In a food processor or blender, combine the oil, vinegar, egg substitute, mustard, tarragon, salt, and pepper. Blend until smooth.

▶ In a small bowl combine the pear, lemon juice, and water. Soak the pear for a couple of minutes to prevent it from darkening. Remove water and pat dry. In another bowl, combine the spinach leaves, fennel, mushrooms, and pear. Pour the dressing over the top and sprinkle on the bacon bits. Serve 1 ounce cold cuts on the side to make up missing protein blocks.

Half of this recipe equals 1 serving.

BLOCKS PER SERVING:	
CARBS:	2
PROTEIN:	1
FAT:	2

TOSSED BROCCOLI AND CAULIFLOWER SALAD

Two servings

Here is a magical salad that can double as a side dish if you par-boil the broccoli and cauliflower and serve everything warm.

2 cups broccoli florets
2 cups cauliflower florets
2 scallions, white parts only, chopped
1 clove garlic, minced
1 cup low-fat yogurt
1 teaspoon Dijon-style mustard
1 tablespoon white wine vinegar
1 teaspoon dried tarragon
2 tablespoons fresh parsley
$1\frac{1}{2}$ scant teaspoons olive oil
Salt and pepper
$\frac{1}{4}$ red bell pepper, chopped
$\frac{1}{4}$ cup grated Parmesan cheese

▶ Combine the broccoli, cauliflower, and onion in a bowl and toss well to mix. Put the garlic, yogurt, mustard, vinegar, tarragon, parsley, and oil in a food processor or blender and whirl until smooth and creamy. Add salt and pepper to taste. Pour over the mixed vegetables and toss to coat. Sprinkle on the bell pepper and cheese to garnish.

Half of this recipe equals 1 serving.

BLOCKS PER SERVING:	
CARBS:	2
PROTEIN:	2
FAT:	2

BALANCED MINESTRONE SOUP

Eight servings

This soup is a great comfort food for wet and cold winter days.

1 tablespoon flour
Salt and pepper
1 pound lean beef, cubed
3 scant teaspoons olive oil, divided
2 cups chopped onions
4 cloves garlic, minced
4 cups chopped celery
2 cups spinach leaves
1 cup thinly sliced carrots
1 cup tomato purée
1/2 cup canned chickpeas
6 cups low-fat chicken stock
1 teaspoon dried basil
1 teaspoon dried oregano
1/2 cup cooked macaroni

▶ Place the flour, salt and pepper, in a large plastic bag, add the beef, and shake until it is coated evenly with the mixture. Heat half the oil in a large skillet over medium heat and brown the beef on all sides. Remove the meat and wipe the skillet clean. Add the rest of the oil to the skillet and sauté the onions and garlic until the onions are soft. Transfer to a large stockpot and combine with the other ingredients (except the pasta).

▶ Cook over medium heat until the soup comes to a slow boil. Reduce the heat to low, and simmer for 35 to 45 minutes. Add the pasta and serve.

Two cups of this soup equals 1 serving.

BLOCKS PER SERVING:	
CARBS:	2
PROTEIN:	2
FAT:	1

BEEF VEGETABLE SOUP

Eight servings

1 tablespoon flour
Salt and pepper
1 pound lean beef, cubed
3 scant teaspoons olive oil, divided
2 cups chopped onions
4 cloves garlic, minced
2 cups diced carrots
5 cups diced celery
4 cups chopped tomatoes
6 cups beef stock
1 cup tomato sauce
1 teaspoon Worcestershire sauce
$1/2$ teaspoon dried marjoram
$1/2$ teaspoon dried oregano
$1/4$ cup minced fresh parsley
2 teaspoons dried chives
$1/8$ cup pearled barley

▶ Combine the flour, salt and pepper, in a large plastic bag. Add the beef and shake until it is coated evenly with the mixture. Heat half the oil over medium heat in a large skillet and brown the beef on all sides. Remove the meat and wipe out the skillet. Add the rest of the oil to the skillet, stir in the onions and garlic, and sauté until the onions are soft.

▶ Add all the ingredients (except the barley) to a large stock pot and bring to a slow boil over medium heat. Reduce the heat and simmer for 20 minutes. Add the barley and cook for another 30 minutes, or until the barley and the beef cubes are tender.

Two and one half cups of this soup equals 1 serving.

BLOCKS PER SERVING:	
CARBS:	2
PROTEIN:	2
FAT:	1

DINNER

One of the hardest adjustments I had to make when I changed my diet was getting over the idea that dinner wasn't pig-out time. I was at a point where I resembled that guy on television, who gets up from the dinner table, undoes his belt and top button of his pants, and falls in front of the television in a stupor.

But just because I cut back on the quantity of food I ate, I didn't want to cut back on the quality of the meal. I like rich sauces and sizzling beef, pork, and chicken.

I found I had to cook with much less oil. So like me, you will have to learn to sauté over low or medium heat, use good non-stick pans, and make cooking spray your best friend.

In most of my recipes I have used natural ingredients, eggs, butter, milk. Imitations just don't give the same results. I want food to be fresh and full of flavor and I use spices liberally. Treat yourself—buy the freshest seafood and vegetables, good quality lean beef and pork, the freshest chicken and poultry. Cook the food as soon as possible after purchasing it.

The recipes in this book can be expanded to feed any number of people. But remember to start with the seasoning called for in the recipe, and add more in small amounts until you are satisfied.

PAN-GRILLED STEAK AND MUSHROOMS

One serving

This dish needs a good cut of beef. Look for good lean meat and spend some time trimming off the excess fat. The salad and apple are a perfect accompaniment to this meal, but if you prefer, serve steamed fresh vegetables instead.

1 teaspoon canola oil
4 ounces lean beef
$^1/_2$ cup thinly sliced onion
$1^1/_2$ cups sliced mushrooms
Pepper
2 teaspoons Worcestershire sauce
1 teaspoon Dijon-style mustard
3 cups lettuce greens with 2 tablespoons
    non-fat dressing
1 apple, peeled, cored, and cut into slices

▶ In a large skillet over medium-high heat, heat the oil and add the beef. Cook for 1 minute on each side to sear the meat. Reduce the heat to medium. Add the onions, mushrooms, pepper, Worcestershire sauce, and mustard. Cook for 2 to 3 minutes, or until the onions are soft. Turn the steak frequently. Remove it to a plate and pour the mushroom mixture over the top. Put the salad to one side and garnish with the apple slices.

BLOCKS PER SERVING:	
CARBS:	4
PROTEIN:	4
FAT:	4

BEEF BURGUNDY

Two servings

8 ounces lean boneless sirloin
$\frac{1}{2}$ cup dry red wine
1 beef bouillon cube
1 cup boiling water
2 shallots, minced
2 cloves garlic, minced
$\frac{1}{2}$ teaspoon dried thyme
$\frac{1}{8}$ teaspoon white pepper
1 scant tablespoon olive oil
3 cups sliced mushrooms
1 cup sliced onions
1 cup chopped tomato
2 teaspoons cornstarch
2 tablespoons cognac
Fresh parsley
2 cups fresh cooked yellow squash or zucchini

▶ Cut the beef across the grain into $\frac{1}{8}$-inch slices. Marinate it in the red wine for 1 hour. Combine the bouillon cube and boiling water. Pour $\frac{1}{4}$ cup over the steak and wine. Save the remainder for another use. Stir in the shallots, garlic, thyme, and pepper. Let stand at room temperature for at least 30 minutes.

▶ Remove the meat, reserving the marinade. In a heavy bottomed skillet, heat the oil over medium heat. Add the mushrooms and onions and sauté, stirring, until the onions are tender. Add the meat and cook, stirring, until it is no longer pink. Mix in the tomatoes and the reserved marinade. Cook, stirring, until the mixture comes to a boil. Dissolve the cornstarch in the cognac and stir into the beef mixture. Cook, stirring, until slightly thickened. Garnish with the parsley and serve with the squash on the side.

Half of this recipe equals 1 serving.

BLOCKS PER SERVING:	
CARBS:	4
PROTEIN:	4
FAT:	4

ONE-SKILLET BEEF STEW

One serving

For a spicier version of this one-pot meal add a little cayenne or red pepper flakes.

$1^1/_2$ scant teaspoons olive oil
$^1/_2$ cup chopped onion
1 clove garlic, minced
1 green bell pepper, seeded and chopped
4 ounces lean beef, cubed
$^1/_2$ cup chopped zucchini
$^1/_2$ cup chopped carrot
1 cup sliced mushrooms
$^1/_2$ cup tomato sauce
$^1/_4$ cup water
1 tablespoon Worcestershire sauce
$^1/_4$ teaspoon dried thyme
Salt and pepper
1 teaspoon minced fresh parsley

▶ Heat the oil in a large skillet over medium heat. Add the onion and garlic and cook for 2 minutes. Add the bell pepper and cook for 3 minutes. Stir in the beef and cook, 4 to 5 minutes. Add the remaining ingredients and stir well. Bring to a slow boil, reduce the heat to low, and simmer for 20 to 30 minutes. Add more water, if needed. Garnish with the parsley.

BLOCKS PER SERVING:	
CARBS:	4
PROTEIN:	4
FAT:	4

MARINATED STEAK KEBAB

—————————— ❧ ——————————

One serving

These kebabs can be done in the broiler, but I prefer to cook them on an outdoor grill with assorted vegetables. Make up a bunch for a balanced party in the fresh air.

1$\frac{1}{2}$ scant teaspoons canola oil
1 teaspoon Worcestershire sauce
1 shallot, minced
1 clove garlic, minced
Dash Tabasco sauce
Salt and pepper
4 ounces lean beef, cubed
$\frac{1}{2}$ green bell pepper, cut into three pieces
2 cherry tomatoes
$\frac{1}{2}$ small onion, cut in half
3 large mushrooms
$\frac{1}{2}$ cup hot cooked rice

▶ Combine the oil, Worcestershire sauce, shallot, garlic, Tabasco, salt and pepper in a bowl. Add the beef and marinate for 4 hours to overnight.

▶ Preheat the oven broiler or prepare the outdoor grill.

▶ Place the beef, green pepper, tomatoes, onion, and mushrooms on a skewer. Place on a rack in a baking dish and cook 6 inches from the heat for 3 minutes on each side for medium rare. On an outdoor grill place the kebabs 6 inches over the heat, turning frequently for about 5 minutes for medium rare. Serve over the rice.

BLOCKS PER SERVING:	
CARBS:	4
PROTEIN:	4
FAT:	4

PEPPERS AND BEEF STIR-FRY

One serving

This great stir-fry is equally good with pork or chicken.

4 ounces lean beef, cut into strips
2 teaspoons cornstarch
1½ scant teaspoons dark sesame oil
½ onion, thinly sliced
2 cloves garlic, minced
¼ teaspoon grated fresh ginger
Pinch red pepper flakes
2 teaspoons low-sodium soy sauce
2 teaspoons rice wine
3 cups thinly sliced mushrooms
1 green bell pepper, seeded and sliced
1 red bell pepper, seeded and sliced
2 cups fresh bean sprouts

▶ Put the beef and cornstarch in a large plastic bag and shake until the beef is well coated. Set aside.

▶ In a large skillet or wok, heat the oil over medium-high heat until hot but not smoking. Reduce the heat to medium. Add the onion, garlic, and ginger. Sauté for 2 minutes. Add the beef and red pepper flakes and cook until the beef is cooked through, about 5 minutes. Stir in the soy sauce, rice wine, and mushrooms. Cook for 3 or 4 minutes, or until the mushrooms are soft. Add the peppers and cook until they start to soften, about 3 minutes. Add the sprouts and cook for 3 minutes longer. Serve hot.

BLOCKS PER SERVING:	
CARBS:	4
PROTEIN:	4
FAT:	4

STEAK WITH A MUSTARD PEPPERCORN SAUCE

Two servings

For this dish make sure to buy good beef and trim it well. When cooking with wine remember the rule: "If you wouldn't drink it, don't cook with it."

1 scant tablespoon olive oil
2 4-ounce beef tenderloins
Salt and white pepper
$^1/_2$ cup dry white wine
1 tablespoon Dijon-style mustard
$^1/_2$ teaspoon Worcestershire sauce
$^1/_2$ tablespoon green peppercorns

▶ Heat the oil in a small skillet over medium heat. Salt and pepper the steak, add it to the hot pan, and sear it for three minutes on each side. Reduce the heat to low and cook for 3 more minutes on each side for medium rare. Transfer it to a cutting board and cover to keep warm.

▶ Increase the heat to high and add the wine. Stir and scrape up any brown bits left in the pan. Add the mustard, Worcestershire sauce, and peppercorns. Cook for two minutes. Cut the steak into thin slices. Arrange on a serving platter, pour on the sauce, and serve immediately. Make up the missing carbohydrate blocks for 1 person with 2 cups tossed salad and 1 cup Brussels sprouts on the side.

Half of this recipe equals 1 serving.

BLOCKS PER SERVING:	
CARBS:	1
PROTEIN:	4
FAT:	4

MARINATED FLANK STEAK

Three servings

1 cup low-sodium soy sauce
2 tablespoons Hoisin sauce
1 tablespoon canola oil
$^1/_2$ cup sweet vermouth
3 tablespoons lemon juice
2 teaspoons Worcestershire sauce
$^1/_2$ teaspoon Tabasco
4 cloves garlic
2 teaspoons Dijon-style mustard
$^1/_2$ teaspoon pepper
10 ounces flank steak, trimmed

▶ Put all the ingredients except the flank steak in a food processor or blender. Blend on high until the marinade is smooth and creamy.

▶ Combine the flank steak with the marinade, cover, and chill. If the steak has already been tenderized, or for any tenderized flank steak from your butcher, marinate it for just 3 hours. Otherwise, let the beef marinate for 12 hours to overnight.

▶ Preheat the oven broiler. Place the meat on a rack in a roasting pan and set 6 inches from the heat. Broil for 5 minutes per side for medium rare. Transfer to a cutting board and slice the steak against the grain into thin pieces.

▶ Pour the remaining marinade into a saucepan along with any of the pan drippings and cook over high heat until the sauce is reduced and somewhat thickened. Pour over the steak and serve. Make up the missing carbohydrate blocks for 1 person with $^1/_2$ cup cooked lentils on the side.

One third of this recipe equals 1 serving.

BLOCKS PER SERVING:	
CARBS:	1
PROTEIN:	3
FAT:	3

BALANCED CHILI BEANS

Three servings

I like my food really spicy and strong flavored. Here is a hearty chili. For a milder version cut back on the chili powder and red pepper flakes.

1 teaspoon canola oil
$^1/_2$ cup chopped onion
2 cloves garlic, minced
1 green bell pepper, seeded, and chopped
$^1/_2$ teaspoon ground cumin
$^1/_2$ teaspoon dried oregano
1 teaspoon chili powder
$^1/_4$ teaspoon red pepper flakes
9 ounces lean ground beef (15% fat)
1 cup tomato sauce
$^1/_3$ cup cooked black beans
$^1/_2$ cup cooked kidney beans
9 black olives, pitted and chopped
Salt and pepper
Fresh cilantro

▶ Heat the oil in a large skillet over medium heat. Add the onion, garlic, green pepper, oregano, and spices. Sauté for 2 minutes, or until the onions begin to soften. Add the ground beef and cook until it is cooked through, breaking up any big pieces with the back of a spoon. Stir in the tomato sauce, the beans, and the olives. When the mixture begins to simmer, reduce the heat to low and simmer for 25 to 30 minutes, adding water if needed. Taste and adjust the seasonings. Transfer to individual serving bowls and garnish with cilantro.

One third of this recipe equals 1 serving.

BLOCKS PER SERVING:	
CARBS:	2
PROTEIN:	3
FAT:	2

SPICY STUFFED PEPPERS

One serving

Double or triple this recipe for a balanced dinner party or for having some extra on hand to make a quick, balanced microwaved snack.

2 green bell peppers
$1^1/_2$ scant teaspoons canola oil
$4^1/_2$ ounces lean ground beef (15% fat)
1 cup chopped onion
2 cloves garlic, minced
1 cup chopped tomato
$^1/_2$ cup spicy salsa (page 14)
$^1/_8$ teaspoon ground nutmeg
$^1/_4$ teaspoon dried thyme
$^1/_4$ teaspoon dried basil
Salt and pepper
3 tablespoons grated cheddar cheese
1 teaspoon minced fresh parsley, divided

▶ Preheat the oven to 350° F.

▶ Cut off the tops of the peppers and clean out the seeds and membrane. Parboil them for 3 to 4 minutes in a large pot of boiling water. Remove them from the pot, drain, and cool.

▶ Heat the oil in a large skillet over medium heat. Add the ground beef, onion, and garlic. Cook until the beef is cooked through, breaking up any large pieces with the back of a spoon. Add the tomatoes, salsa, and spices. Cook, stirring until the mixture is well combined and heated through. Pour off any excess fat and stuff the peppers with the meat mixture. Sprinkle the grated cheese over the top and set in a deep baking dish. Pour in enough water to come half way up the sides of the peppers. Bake for 30 minutes. Garnish with the parsley.

BLOCKS PER SERVING:	
CARBS:	4
PROTEIN:	4
FAT:	4

KEEMA MATER
(Indian Spiced Beef)

Three servings

Use your own judgment on the amount of cayenne.

1 pound lean ground beef
2 teaspoons canola oil
2 cups chopped onions
2 cloves garlic, minced
2 cups V-8 juice
²/₃ cup peas (fresh or frozen)
Salt
¼ teaspoon pepper
⅛ teaspoon ground cumin
⅛ teaspoon cumin seeds
⅛ teaspoon ground coriander
⅛ to ¼ teaspoon cayenne
¼ teaspoon garam masala (page 12)
½ cup cooked basmati rice
2 tablespoons non-fat sour cream
12 roasted peanuts, chopped

▶ In a large skillet, heat oil over medium-high heat. Add the beef, cook for 2 minutes, and stir in the onions. Continue cooking until the meat is cooked through, crumbling it with a fork. Pour off any fat and add the V-8 juice and peas. Reduce the heat and simmer for 3 minutes, or until the peas are cooked through. Remove from the heat and keep warm.

▶ In a small skillet, over medium heat, combine the salt, pepper, cumin, cumin seeds, coriander, and cayenne. Stir and cook for 1 minute. Add the garam masala and stir well. Add the spices to the beef mixture and the cooked rice. Garnish with the sour cream and peanuts.

One third of the recipe equals 1 serving.

BLOCKS PER SERVING:	
CARBS:	3
PROTEIN:	3
FAT:	3

PORK TENDERLOIN WITH A MUSTARD SAUCE

Three servings

8 fresh sage leaves, minced, divided
1/4 cup stone-ground mustard, divided
White pepper, divided
2 cloves garlic, minced, divided
3 scallions, white parts only, minced, divided
10 ounces pork tenderloin, fat removed
1 tablespoon olive oil, divided
1/2 cup dry white wine
2 shallots, minced
1/2 cup 1% milk
2 teaspoons cornstarch
1/4 cup water

▶ Mix the sage, half the mustard, pepper, garlic, and scallions. Put the pork on a plate and spread the mustard mixture over the top. Cover, and chill for at least 4 hours to overnight.

▶ Preheat the oven to 375° F.

▶ Place the pork on a rack in a pan. Drizzle on half the oil. Bake for 20 to 25 minutes, or until the pork is cooked through. Baste every 5 minutes with the white wine.

▶ Meanwhile, heat the rest of the oil in a skillet over low heat. Sauté the shallots until wilted. Add the milk and any remaining wine; bring to a simmer. Stir the cornstarch into the milk mixture. Stir constantly until the sauce thickens. Add the remaining mustard mixture and 2 tablespoons of the pan juices; mix well. Adjust the seasoning and keep warm.

▶ When the pork is done, remove it from the oven and let stand for 10 minutes. Slice the pork thin, pour the sauce over the roast, and serve. Make up the missing carbohydrate blocks for 1 person with 2 cups tossed salad and 1 cup cooked broccoli on the side.

One third of this recipe is 1 serving.

BLOCKS PER SERVING:	
CARBS:	1
PROTEIN:	3
FAT:	3

PORK TENDERLOIN WITH GARLIC AND MUSHROOMS

Three servings

9 ounces pork tenderloin, cut into thin slices
2 tablespoons flour
$\frac{1}{2}$ teaspoon ground ginger
Salt and pepper
1 scant tablespoon olive oil
3 cloves garlic, minced
6 cups sliced mushrooms
6 tablespoons dry sherry
Fresh parsley, chopped

▶ Place the pork between sheets of wax paper and flatten to $\frac{1}{4}$-inch with a mallet. Combine the flour, ginger, salt and pepper. Dredge the pork with this mixture.

▶ Heat the oil in a large skillet. Add the garlic and cook until it begins to soften, about 1 minute. Remove from the skillet with a slotted spoon, and set aside.

▶ Add the pork to the skillet and sauté about 3 minutes per side. Remove from the pan, and keep warm.

▶ Add the mushrooms to the skillet and cook for 4 minutes. Increase the heat to medium-high and add the sherry. Boil until the mixture thickens, about 6 minutes. Stir in the garlic. Spoon the mushroom sauce over the pork, garnish with the parsley, and serve. Make up the missing carbohydrate blocks for 1 person with 2 cups cooked yellow squash on the side.

One third of this recipe equals 1 serving.

BLOCKS PER SERVING:	
CARBS:	1
PROTEIN:	3
FAT:	3

PORK SCALLOPINE

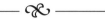

Three servings

10 ounces pork tenderloin, cut into slices
2 tablespoons flour
Salt and pepper
1 tablespoon olive oil, divided
2 cloves garlic, minced
$\frac{1}{2}$ teaspoon crushed dried rosemary
$\frac{1}{4}$ cup sweet vermouth
$\frac{1}{4}$ cup vegetable stock (page 14)
4 plum tomatoes, chopped
1 tablespoon lemon zest
3 cups sliced mushrooms
3 black olives, chopped

▶ Place the slices of pork between two pieces of plastic wrap or wax paper and pound with a rolling pin or mallet. Flatten to $\frac{1}{4}$-inch thickness. In a bowl, combine the flour, salt, and pepper. Dredge the pork with the flour mixture.

▶ Heat $\frac{3}{4}$ tablespoon of the oil in a large skillet over medium heat and sauté the pork about 3 minutes on each side, or until done through and nicely browned. Remove the pork, arrange on a serving platter, and keep warm.

▶ Reduce the heat to low and add the rest of the oil to the skillet. Add the garlic and rosemary and cook, stirring, for 1 minute. Stir in the wine and increase the heat to high. Bring to a boil and cook, stirring and scraping up any brown bits. Cook until the liquid is reduced to a glaze, about 3 minutes. Add the stock and boil to reduce to about half. Add the tomatoes, mushrooms, and lemon zest. Cook and stir for about 3 minutes, or until the mushrooms are soft. Add the olives and cook 1 minute longer. Adjust the seasoning and spoon over the pork.

One third of this recipe equals 1 serving.

BLOCKS PER SERVING:	
CARBS:	3
PROTEIN:	3
FAT:	3

PORK TENDERLOIN IN A WHITE WINE SAUCE

Three servings

10 ounces pork tenderloin, trimmed and cut into
   $1/2$-inch slices
2 tablespoons flour
Salt and pepper
2 teaspoons canola oil
$1^{1}/_{2}$ scant teaspoons butter
1 shallot, sliced
3 cups sliced mushrooms
$1/4$ teaspoon crushed dried rosemary
$1/3$ cup dry white wine
$1/4$ cup vegetable stock
1 teaspoon chopped fresh parsley

▶ Combine the pork, flour, salt and pepper, in a large plastic bag. Shake until the pork is evenly coated with the flour. Remove the pork from the bag and shake off the excess flour.

▶ Heat the oil in a large skillet over medium heat. Add the butter and stir until it melts. Add the pork and shallot. Cook, stirring occasionally, for 4 minutes. Turn the pork over and add the mushrooms. Cook for 4 minutes more, remove the pork to a serving platter, and keep warm.

▶ Add the wine and stock to the skillet. Increase the heat to high and bring to a boil. Cook, stirring, until the mixture is reduced by half. Pour over the pork, garnish with the parsley, and serve. Make up the missing carbohydrate blocks for 1 person with 2 cups tossed green salad and 1 cup sautéed mushrooms on the side.

One third of this recipe equals 1 serving.

BLOCKS PER SERVING:	
CARBS:	1
PROTEIN:	3
FAT:	3

PORK AND RED CHILI STIR-FRY

Three servings

For this zesty dish, you can use chicken or beef instead of pork if you prefer. Because I like my food on the spicy side, I add more pepper flakes and a dash of cayenne.

2 teaspoons canola oil
10 ounces pork tenderloin, cut in strips
3 cloves garlic, minced
2 cups cut green beans, fresh or frozen
2 teaspoons sugar
3 teaspoons low-sodium soy sauce
1/2 teaspoon or more red chili flakes
2 teaspoons minced fresh ginger
1 teaspoon dark sesame oil (page 11)
1 teaspoon rice vinegar
1 cup hot cooked rice

▶ Heat the oil in a wok or large skillet over medium-high heat. Reduce the heat to medium. Add the pork and garlic and cook for 2 minutes, or until the pork is cooked through. Add the green beans and cook for 2 minutes, or until they are tender. Push the pork and beans to the sides of the wok and add the rest of the ingredients in the center. Stir and cook for 1 minute. Spoon over the rice.

One third of this recipe equals 1 serving.

BLOCKS PER SERVING:	
CARBS:	3
PROTEIN:	3
FAT:	3

STIR-FRY CHICKEN HOISIN

Two servings

2 tablespoons Hoisin sauce (page 10)
2 scant teaspoons dark sesame oil (page 11)
1 tablespoon low-sodium soy sauce
2 cloves garlic, minced
2 tablespoons chopped scallions, green parts only
1 tablespoon honey
¼ teaspoon salt
8 ounces boneless skinless chicken, cut into strips
1 teaspoon canola oil
½ cup thinly sliced carrots
1 cup thinly sliced onion
1 cup cooked rice

▶ Combine the Hoisin sauce, sesame oil, soy sauce, garlic, scallions, honey, and salt in a bowl. Add the chicken and marinate for at least 2 hours in the refrigerator.

▶ Heat the oil in a wok or skillet over medium heat. Add the carrots and cook for 5 minutes. Remove the chicken from the marinade with a slotted spoon. Add it to the wok and stir-fry until it is almost cooked through, about 4 minutes. Stir in the onion and the reserved marinade. Cook until the onions are soft and the liquid is bubbling, about 3 minutes. Serve with the rice on the side.

One half of this recipe equals 1 serving.

BLOCKS PER SERVING:	
CARBS:	4
PROTEIN:	4
FAT:	4

CHICKEN OR PORK AMANDINE

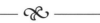

Three servings

This dish is close to perfect as is, but if you don't mind cheating a little on the fat blocks, adding more almonds can make this dish even better.

10 ounces boneless chicken, cut into strips, or
   10 ounces pork tenderloin, cut into slices
Salt and pepper
2 tablespoons flour
1 egg white
2 tablespoons water
2 teaspoons chopped almonds
$^1/_2$ scant teaspoon butter
$2^1/_2$ scant teaspoons canola oil
$^1/_2$ fresh lime

▶ Place the chicken or pork pieces between two sheet of wax paper and flatten to about $^1/_4$-inch with a mallet or rolling pin. Season each piece with salt and pepper. Dredge with the flour, one piece at a time, and shake off the excess. Combine the egg white and water and beat with a wire whisk until mixed thoroughly. Dip the floured chicken or pork in the egg, letting the excess drip off. Arrange the pieces on a baking sheet lined with wax paper. Sprinkle with the almonds and chill for 1 hour.

▶ In a skillet, heat the oil over medium heat and add the butter. Sauté the chicken or pork for 2 minutes on each side, or until deep golden and done through. Transfer the meat to a paper towel to drain. Arrange on a serving plate, squeeze a little fresh lime juice over the top, and serve. Make up the missing carbohydrate blocks for 1 person with $^1/_2$ cup streamed rice on the side.

One third of this recipe equals 1 serving.

BLOCKS PER SERVING:	
CARBS:	$^1/_3$
PROTEIN:	3
FAT:	3

ORANGE-GINGER CHICKEN

Two servings

The marmalade gives this recipe a wonderful flavor. Increase the red pepper flakes if you like a little more heat in your food.

3 tablespoons orange marmalade
$\frac{1}{2}$ tablespoon Dijon-style mustard
1 teaspoon minced fresh ginger
$\frac{1}{2}$ scant teaspoon dark sesame oil (page 11)
Pinch red pepper flakes
8 ounces boneless, skinless chicken, cut into strips
$\frac{1}{2}$ tablespoon butter, melted
$\frac{1}{2}$ teaspoon fresh orange zest
$\frac{1}{8}$ teaspoon ground ginger

▶ Combine the marmalade, mustard, ginger, oil, and red pepper in a bowl. Add the chicken and turn to coat. Cover and chill for 2 or 3 hours.

▶ Preheat the oven to 350° F.

▶ Arrange the chicken on a wire rack in a baking dish or roasting pan. Bake for 10 to 12 minutes, or until it is done through. Baste the chicken with the drippings 2 or 3 times while cooking.

▶ Combine the butter, orange zest, and ginger in a small bowl, stirring to blend. Spoon this butter mixture over the chicken and serve. Make up the missing carbohydrate blocks for 1 person with $\frac{1}{2}$ cup steamed rice on the side.

One half of this recipe equals 1 serving.

BLOCKS PER SERVING:	
CARBS:	2
PROTEIN:	4
FAT:	4

HONEY-SOY CHICKEN

Two servings

The easy chicken dish gets its special flavor from the soy sauce, honey, and sherry combination that makes the base for this wonderful Oriental sauce.

$\frac{1}{3}$ **cup low-sodium soy sauce**
2$\frac{1}{2}$ tablespoons honey
2 tablespoons dry sherry
2 cloves garlic, minced
1$\frac{1}{2}$ teaspoons dark sesame oil (page 11)
8 ounces boneless, skinless chicken breast
2 teaspoons dry roasted sesame seeds
1 teaspoon minced scallions
1 cup hot cooked rice

▶ Combine the soy sauce, honey, sherry, garlic, and sesame oil in a large bowl. Add the chicken, cover, and chill overnight, turning occasionally.

▶ Drain the sauce into a saucepan and over medium heat slowly bring to a boil. Reduce the heat to simmer and add the chicken. Cook for about 15 to 20 minutes, or until the chicken is cooked through but tender. Divide it into two portions, transfer it to a plate, and drip on half the sauce. Sprinkle on the sesame seeds, top with the scallions, and serve with the rice.

One half of this recipe equals 1 serving.

BLOCKS PER SERVING:	
CARBS:	4
PROTEIN:	4
FAT:	4

BALANCED TANDOORI CHICKEN

Two servings

Although not quite the same as clay pot cooking, this is not too far off from the original.

8 ounces boneless, skinless chicken
2 tablespoons fresh lime juice
¼ cup low-fat yogurt
2 cloves garlic, minced
1 tablespoon canola oil
1 teaspoon ground cumin
1 teaspoon chili powder
1 teaspoon minced fresh ginger
½ teaspoon paprika
¼ teaspoon salt
½ teaspoon ground turmeric
4 tablespoons chopped dry roasted peanuts
1½ cups hot cooked basmati rice

▶ Wash the chicken and pat it dry. Combine the remaining ingredients, except the rice, in a bowl and mix well. Add the chicken and turn to coat. Transfer it to a lightly greased baking dish, cover, and refrigerate for at least 2 hours to overnight.

▶ Preheat the oven to 400° F.

▶ Roast the chicken, covered, for 15 minutes, turn, and roast it for an additional 15 minutes. Reduce the oven temperature to 350°, pour off any fat, turn the chicken, and cook for 15 minutes longer. Transfer to a cutting board and slice it into strips. Arrange on a serving platter, sprinkle the peanuts over the top, and serve with the rice.

One half of this recipe equals 1 serving.

BLOCKS PER SERVING:	
CARBS:	4
PROTEIN:	4
FAT:	4

CHICKEN WITH FRESH BASIL AND OLIVES

Two servings

My roommate brought this wonderful recipe back from Thailand, where he lived for several years. I borrowed it from him and changed it just a little to balance it. It is equally wonderful with pork.

2 teaspoons olive oil
2 cloves garlic, minced
1 cup chopped fresh basil, divided
1 serrano chili, stemmed, seeded, and sliced
8 ounces boneless, skinless chicken
1 tablespoon Asian fish sauce
2 tablespoons water
2 teaspoons sugar
6 black olives, pitted and chopped
1 cup cooked jasmine rice

▶ Heat the oil in a large skillet or wok over medium heat. Add the garlic and sauté until golden brown, about 1 minute. Add half the basil and all the chili and stir-fry until the basil is wilted, about 1 minute. Add the chicken and stir-fry until it is almost cooked through, 5 to 7 minutes. Stir in the fish sauce, water, and sugar. Cook until the sauce bubbles and thickens slightly, about 2 minutes. Add the rest of the basil and the olives. Cook until the basil is wilted, about 30 seconds. Serve immediately with the rice. Make up the missing carbohydrate blocks for 1 person with 1 small steamed artichoke on the side.

One half of this recipe equals 1 serving.

BLOCKS PER SERVING:	
CARBS:	3
PROTEIN:	4
FAT:	4

CHICKEN WITH A LEMON-BASIL SAUCE

Two servings

Lemon and basil are perfect accompaniments to this simple chicken dish.

1 tablespoon olive oil
2 boneless, skinless chicken breasts,
   4 to 5 ounces each
Salt and pepper
1 tablespoon fresh lemon juice
2 cloves garlic, chopped
$\frac{1}{2}$ teaspoon lemon zest
$\frac{1}{2}$ cup low-fat chicken stock
$\frac{1}{4}$ cup chopped fresh basil

▶ Heat the oil in a skillet over medium heat. Sprinkle the chicken with salt and pepper. Add it to the skillet and sauté until brown and cooked through, about 6 minutes per side. Transfer to a serving platter and keep warm.

▶ Add the lemon juice, garlic, and zest to the same skillet. Keeping the medium heat, stir for 30 seconds, or until fragrant. Add the chicken stock, increase the heat, and boil until reduced to sauce consistency, about 5 minutes. Stir the basil into the sauce. Taste and adjust the seasoning, if needed, and spoon over the chicken. Make up the missing carbohydrate blocks for 1 person with 2 cups tossed salad and $\frac{1}{2}$ cup cooked pasta on the side.

One half of this recipe equals 1 serving.

BLOCKS PER SERVING:	
CARBS:	$\frac{1}{2}$
PROTEIN:	$4\frac{1}{2}$
FAT:	$4\frac{1}{2}$

SZECHUAN CHICKEN

Two servings

Here is a balanced version of a Chinese classic. If you like, add more cayenne to heat it up a bit.

3 tablespoons low-sodium soy sauce
1 tablespoon white wine vinegar
1 teaspoon dark sesame oil (page 11)
1 teaspoon sugar
$^1/_2$ teaspoon cayenne
8 ounces boneless, skinless chicken, diced
1 tablespoon cornstarch
2 scant teaspoons canola oil
3 cloves garlic, minced
Pinch red pepper flakes
2 scallions, sliced
$1^1/_2$ cups hot cooked rice

▶ Combine the soy sauce, vinegar, sesame oil, sugar, and cayenne in a bowl and set aside. Shake the chicken and the cornstarch together in a plastic bag.

▶ Heat the oil in a wok or skillet over medium heat. Add the chicken and garlic and stir-fry until the chicken is cooked through. Add the soy sauce mixture and stir-fry for 1 minute.

▶ Remove the chicken with a slotted spoon to a serving dish. Increase the heat to high. Stir the sauce for 1 minute and then add the scallions. Cook for 1 minute longer or until thickened. Pour the sauce over the chicken and serve it immediately with the rice.

One half of this recipe equals 1 serving.

BLOCKS PER SERVING:	
CARBS:	4
PROTEIN:	4
FAT:	4

CHICKEN WITH A TARRAGON-CAPER SAUCE

Two servings

I love capers. Whenever a recipe calls for them, it makes me happy. This sauce goes equally well over grilled pork.

8 ounces boneless, skinless chicken, cut into pieces
Salt and pepper
1 teaspoon olive oil
4 teaspoons capers
$\frac{1}{2}$ teaspoon fresh lemon juice
$\frac{1}{2}$ teaspoon dried tarragon
$1\frac{1}{2}$ teaspoons butter
$\frac{1}{2}$ teaspoon chopped fresh parsley

▶ Place the pieces of chicken between two sheets of wax paper and flatten with a mallet or rolling pin. Pat dry and season with salt and pepper. Heat the oil in a skillet over medium heat. Add the chicken and cook through, about 5 minutes per side. Transfer it to a serving platter and keep warm.

▶ Wipe the skillet clean and add the capers, lemon juice, and tarragon. Bring to a boil and remove from the heat. Add the butter and stir the sauce until the butter is melted and combined with the rest of the ingredients. Pour over the chicken, sprinkle on the parsley, and serve. Make up the missing carbohydrate blocks for 1 person with 2 cups tossed green salad and 1 small baked potato on the side.

One half of this recipe equals 1 serving.

BLOCKS PER SERVING:	
CARBS:	0
PROTEIN:	4
FAT:	4

CHICKEN WITH A MUSHROOM-SHERRY SAUCE

Two servings

2 teaspoons butter
1 scant teaspoon canola oil
8 ounces boneless, skinless chicken, cut into strips
1$\frac{1}{2}$ cups sliced mushrooms
2 scallions, green parts only, chopped
Salt and pepper
$\frac{1}{2}$ cup dry sherry
$\frac{1}{2}$ cup vegetable stock (page 14)
$\frac{1}{4}$ teaspoon dried thyme
$\frac{1}{4}$ teaspoon lemon zest
$\frac{1}{2}$ teaspoon chopped fresh parsley
1 cup hot cooked rice

▶ In a skillet, melt half the butter in the oil over medium heat. Add the chicken and sauté until it is cooked through, about 5 minutes. Transfer to a serving plate and keep warm.

▶ Melt the remaining butter in the same skillet over medium heat. Add the mushrooms and onions. Season with salt and pepper. Cook until the mushrooms are tender, about 3 minutes. Add the sherry, stock, thyme, and lemon zest. Bring to a boil, scraping up any brown bits in the skillet. Cook until the sauce has reduced by about a half. Return the chicken to the skillet along with any juices left on the serving plate. Simmer for about 5 minutes. Adjust the seasonings. Transfer again to the serving plate and pour the sauce over the top. Sprinkle on the parsley and serve with the rice.

One half of this recipe equals 1 serving.

BLOCKS PER SERVING:	
CARBS:	4
PROTEIN:	4
FAT:	4

GARLIC-ROASTED CHICKEN

Two servings

Here is a wonderfully aromatic sauce you shouldn't miss.

> 2 boneless, skinless chicken breasts,
>   4 to 5 ounces each
> ¾ teaspoon crumbled dried sage
> Salt and pepper
> 1 tablespoon olive oil
> 1 head garlic, separated into cloves, unpeeled
> ¼ cup dry white wine

▶ Preheat the oven to 400° F.

▶ Sprinkle the chicken with the sage, salt, and pepper. Press the seasonings in with your fingers. Heat the oil in a ovenproof skillet over medium heat. Add the chicken and sauté until brown, about 3 minutes per side.

▶ In a small saucepan boil the garlic in water for 2 minutes, then drain. Let cool and peel.

▶ Arrange the garlic around the chicken in the skillet and add the wine. Cover and bake for 10 minutes. Uncover and baste the chicken with the pan juices. Bake uncovered about 5 minutes, or until the chicken is done through. Transfer it to a serving platter with a slotted spoon. The garlic can be served or discarded.

▶ Boil the pan juices over a high heat until thickened, about 3 minutes. Taste and adjust seasonings and spoon over the chicken. Make up the missing carbohydrate blocks for 1 person with 2 cups tossed green salad and 1 small baked potato on the side.

One half of this recipe equals 1 serving.

BLOCKS PER SERVING:	
CARBS:	1
PROTEIN:	5
FAT:	5

BAKED CHICKEN SUPREME

Two servings

Chicken and pecans are a wonderful combination and the coating adds a neat crunch to this dish.

> 2 tablespoons chopped pecans
> 6 tablespoons dry bread crumbs
> 1 cup low-fat yogurt
> 1 tablespoon fresh lemon juice
> 1/2 teaspoon Worcestershire sauce
> 1/2 teaspoon crushed celery seed
> 1/2 teaspoon paprika, divided
> 1 clove garlic, minced
> Salt and pepper
> 8 ounces boneless, skinless chicken, cut into strips

▶ Blend the pecans and the bread crumbs in a food processor or blender until the pecans are chopped fine. Set aside.

▶ Combine the yogurt, lemon juice, Worcestershire sauce, celery seed, paprika, garlic, salt and pepper, in a bowl. Add the chicken and turn to coat. Cover and chill overnight in the refrigerator.

▶ Preheat the oven to 325° F.

▶ Remove the chicken from the marinade. Discard the marinade. Dredge the chicken in the pecan mixture until well coated. Arrange the strips on a rack in a shallow baking dish. Bake for 15 to 20 minutes, or until the chicken is cooked through and the juices begin to run. Garnish with additional paprika and serve. Make up the missing carbohydrate blocks for 1 person with 2 cups tossed green salad on the side.

One half of this recipe equals 1 serving.

BLOCKS PER SERVING:	
CARBS:	3
PROTEIN:	4 1/2
FAT:	4

BAKED HALIBUT AND YOGURT

Three servings

A good rule to remember for fish dishes is to buy the freshest fish you can find and plan a menu around it, rather than planning a menu and then buying the fish. Halibut usually can be found fresh when you need it.

2 8-ounce halibut steaks
2 tablespoons fresh lemon juice
Salt and pepper
$\frac{1}{2}$ onion, chopped fine
1 serrano chili, seeded and minced
2 cloves garlic, minced
1 teaspoon ground coriander
1 teaspoon minced fresh ginger
$3\frac{1}{2}$ scant teaspoons olive oil
$\frac{1}{2}$ cup low-fat yogurt
1 teaspoon sugar
1 teaspoon chopped roasted almonds

▶ Brush the lemon juice over the fish, lightly salt and pepper it, and let it stand for 10 to 15 minutes.

▶ Mix the onion, chili, garlic, coriander, and ginger in a bowl. Heat the oil in a skillet over medium heat. Add the onion mixture and sauté until golden, about 5 minutes. Add the yogurt and sugar to the skillet, cook until heated through and thick enough to coat the fish.

▶ Preheat the oven to 375° F.

▶ Place the fish on a baking sheet lined with foil and spread the yogurt mixture over the top. Bake for about 9 to 10 minutes, or until the fish is cooked through. Remove from the oven, sprinkle with the almonds, and serve. Make up the missing carbohydrate blocks for 1 person with $\frac{1}{2}$ cup cooked pasta and 1 cup (about 10) cooked asparagus spears.

BLOCKS PER SERVING:	
CARBS:	1
PROTEIN:	4
FAT:	4

One third of this recipe equals 1 serving.

BAKED HALIBUT WITH
RED PEPPERS AND RED ONION

— ❧ —

Three servings

The red bell peppers and orange peel add color and zest to this baked fish dish.

1 red bell pepper, julienned
$\frac{1}{2}$ red onion, julienned
1 tablespoon olive oil
1 tablespoon minced orange peel
1 clove garlic, minced
2 8-ounce halibut steaks
$\frac{1}{2}$ scant teaspoon butter, melted
$\frac{1}{2}$ teaspoon dried thyme
Salt and pepper
1 tablespoon fresh lemon juice

▶ Preheat the oven to 400° F.

▶ Combine the peppers, onion, olive oil, and orange peel and distribute evenly over 13x9-inch baking dish. Bake until the edges of the bell peppers and onion begin to brown, stirring occasionally, about 20 minutes. Mix the garlic into the vegetables, and push to one side.

▶ Brush the fish with the melted butter and arrange in the center of the dish. Sprinkle with the thyme, salt, and pepper. Spoon some of the vegetables on top of the fish. Bake until the fish is opaque, about 10 minutes for each 1 inch of thickness. Drizzle with the lemon juice and serve. Make up the missing carbohydrate blocks for 1 person with 2 cups tossed green salad and 1 cup steamed broccoli on the side.

One third of this recipe equals 1 serving.

BLOCKS PER SERVING:	
CARBS:	1
PROTEIN:	3
FAT:	3

BROILED HALIBUT WITH RED ONION AND DILL

Three servings

This quick and easy dish is equally good with salmon or red snapper.

1 cup finely chopped red onion
2 teaspoons soft butter
1 tablespoon light canola mayonnaise
2 tablespoons fresh lemon juice
3 teaspoon Dijon-style mustard
1 tablespoon chopped fresh dill weed
Salt and pepper
2 8-ounce halibut steaks
3 teaspoons finely chopped dry roasted almonds
Fresh parsley

▶ Preheat the oven broiler.

▶ Combine the onion, butter, mayonnaise, lemon juice, mustard, dill, salt and pepper, and set aside.

▶ Line a baking sheet with foil, and set a rack in the middle of the sheet. Arrange the halibut on the rack. Spread the onion mixture evenly over the fish. Broil the fish about 6 inches from the heat for 6 to 8 minutes. The top should be a golden brown, and the fish should flake easily when tested with a fork.

▶ Remove to a serving platter, sprinkle with the almonds, garnish with parsley, and serve. Make up the missing carbohydrate blocks for 1 person with 2 cups steamed Swiss chard on the side.

One third of this recipe equals 1 serving.

BLOCKS PER SERVING:	
CARBS:	1
PROTEIN:	3
FAT:	3

HALIBUT PROVENCALE

Three servings

For variety, try salmon, or fresh red snapper in this recipe.

2 cups seeded, chopped Roma tomatoes
3 black olives, chopped
1 tablespoon capers
1 tablespoon fresh lemon juice
1 tablespoon olive oil, divided
Salt and pepper
2 8-ounce halibut steaks

▶ Combine the tomatoes, olives, capers, lemon juice, and 2 teaspoons oil in a bowl. Season with salt and pepper.

▶ Preheat the oven to 425° F.

▶ Brush the halibut with the remaining teaspoon of oil and season with additional pepper. Arrange the steak on a rack in a baking dish. Spoon half of the tomato mixture over the top. Bake the fish until just cooked through, about 10 to 12 minutes. Pour the rest of the tomato mixture onto an ovenproof serving plate and heat it in the oven for 1 minute. Arrange the fish on top of the sauce, spoon the pan juices over the fish, and serve. Make up the missing carbohydrate blocks for 1 person with 2 cups tossed green salad and 1 small sliced cucumber.

One third of this recipe equals 1 serving.

BLOCKS PER SERVING:	
CARBS:	1
PROTEIN:	3
FAT:	3

BAKED SALMON WITH TOMATOES, OLIVES, AND FRESH HERBS

Three servings

3 scant teaspoons olive oil
3 cloves garlic, minced, divided
1/2 onion, chopped
2 8-ounce salmon filets
Salt and pepper
1/4 cup chopped fresh basil
2 teaspoons chopped fresh oregano
1 teaspoon chopped fresh mint
1 cup seeded, chopped Roma tomatoes
Pinch red pepper flakes
6 black olives, pitted and chopped
1 tablespoon drained capers

▶ Heat the oil in a large skillet over low heat. Add half the garlic and cook until golden, stirring occasionally. Do not brown. Remove the garlic and reserve. Increase the heat to medium. Add the onion and sauté for 2 minutes. Add the salmon and sear on both sides, about 1 minute per side. Season with salt and pepper. Remove from the heat and arrange the filets side by side in a baking dish.

▶ Preheat the oven to 400° F.

▶ Combine the basil, oregano, and mint. Sprinkle half the mixture over the salmon. Bake for about 10 minutes, or until the salmon has cooked through. Remove from the oven and keep warm.

▶ Place a small skillet over medium-high heat, add the tomatoes and pepper flakes, and sauté for 1 minute. Add the olives, capers, and reserved garlic. Toss to heat through. Spoon this mixture over the salmon, sprinkle with the remaining herbs, and serve. Make up the missing carbohydrate blocks for 1 person with 2 cups tossed green salad and 2 cups steamed zucchini.

One third of this recipe equals 1 serving.

BLOCKS PER SERVING:	
CARBS:	1
PROTEIN:	3
FAT:	3

BROILED SALMON WITH
A MUSTARD VINAIGRETTE

Three servings

This recipe is a delicious way of incorporating EPA (eicosapentaenoic acid) into to your diet.

1 tablespoon olive oil
$1/4$ cup white wine vinegar
2 tablespoons water
$1^1/2$ tablespoons Dijon-style mustard
1 shallot, chopped fine
$1/4$ cup chopped parsley
Salt and pepper
2 8-ounce salmon filets
Cooking spray
1 teaspoon chopped fresh basil
1 teaspoon chopped fresh tarragon

▶ Place the olive oil, vinegar, water, mustard, shallot, parsley, salt and pepper in a food processor or blender. Blend until smooth. Adjust the seasoning with more water, salt and pepper, if needed. Set aside.

▶ Preheat the oven broiler.

▶ Place the fish in a baking dish coated lightly with cooking spray. Lightly spray the top of the fish. Sprinkle on the herbs. Broil the fish for 3 minutes on each side, or until cooked through but still moist. Pour a little of the vinaigrette on a plate, place the fish on top. Drizzle the rest of the vinaigrette over the top and serve. Make up the missing carbohydrate blocks for 1 person with 1 small baked potato on the side.

One third of this recipe equals 1 serving.

BLOCKS PER SERVING:	
CARBS:	1
PROTEIN:	3
FAT:	3

RED SNAPPER STEW

Three servings

Red snapper is common where I live on the coast of California. This simple tasty recipe is a favorite around my house.

1 tablespoon canola oil, divided
3 cloves garlic, sliced
1 pound snapper filets
Salt and pepper
2 cups peeled, seeded, diced tomatoes
1 onion, sliced
½ green bell pepper, sliced
½ red bell pepper, sliced
Scant ½ teaspoon dark sesame oil (page 11)
3 tablespoons fresh lime juice
2 cups cooked pasta

▶ Preheat the oven to 350° F.

▶ Heat half the canola oil in a skillet over medium heat. Add the garlic and sauté until it begins to turn golden, about 1 minute. Spread the cooked garlic and oil evenly over the bottom of a 13x9-inch baking dish. Arrange the fish over the garlic and sprinkle lightly with the salt and pepper. Top with the tomatoes, onion, and bell peppers. Sprinkle again lightly with pepper. Mix the sesame oil with the rest of the canola oil and drizzle it and the lime juice over the top of the fish. Cover with foil and bake until the fish is opaque, about 15 minutes. Serve over the pasta.

One third of this recipe equals 1 serving.

BLOCKS PER SERVING:	
CARBS:	3
PROTEIN:	3
FAT:	3

LINGUINE WITH HOT SHRIMP AND ASPARAGUS

Three servings

The flavor of garlic, red peppers, and shrimp is outstanding in this unusual combination.

1 pound shredded cooked shrimp meat
2 teaspoons lemon juice
3 cloves garlic, crushed and chopped
1/4 teaspoon red pepper flakes
1 can (15 ounces) Italian-style stewed tomatoes
1/2 teaspoon dried oregano
1/2 teaspoon dried basil
24 fresh asparagus spears, about 3 inches long
3 1/2 scant teaspoons olive oil
2 cups cooked linguine

▶ Toss the shrimp, lemon juice, garlic, and red pepper flakes in a bowl. Cover and chill for 15 to 20 minutes.

▶ Combine the tomatoes, oregano, and basil in a saucepan. Cook over medium heat for 15 minutes, stirring and crushing the tomatoes with the back of a spoon.

▶ Sauté the asparagus spears in half the oil in a skillet over medium-high heat until tender, about 4 minutes. Transfer to a bowl and keep warm. Put the cooked pasta in a large serving bowl and keep warm.

▶ Heat the remaining oil in the same pan and add the shrimp mixture. Sauté for 4 minutes or until the shrimp has turned opaque. Stir in the tomato sauce and cook for 1 minute. Toss into the linguine with the asparagus.

One third of this recipe equals 1 serving.

BLOCKS PER SERVING:	
CARBS:	3
PROTEIN:	3
FAT:	3

SCALLOPS WITH WALNUTS AND SHALLOTS

Three servings

For this recipe with a delicate flavor and a little crunch, be sure to buy large fresh scallops that smell sweet, not fishy. Use them immediately to take advantage of their flavor. If you get them frozen, thaw them slowly in the refrigerator.

1 teaspoon butter
1 teaspoon canola oil
$\frac{1}{2}$ cup sliced shallots
Salt and pepper
$\frac{1}{3}$ cup dry white wine
$\frac{1}{4}$ teaspoon dried thyme
13 ounces sea scallops
$1\frac{1}{2}$ teaspoons minced, toasted walnuts
$\frac{1}{4}$ cup chopped flat leaf parsley
$1\frac{1}{2}$ cups cooked rice

▶ Melt the butter and the oil in a skillet over medium heat. Add the shallots, salt, and pepper. Sauté until they are golden brown, about 3 minutes. Add the wine and thyme and cook until the liquid has been reduced by about $\frac{1}{3}$. Add the scallops and stir until just opaque, about 3 to 4 minutes. Mix in the walnuts and parsley and serve on a bed of hot rice.

One third of this recipe equals 1 serving.

BLOCKS PER SERVING:	
CARBS:	3
PROTEIN:	3
FAT:	3

LINGUINE WITH SCALLOPS AND RED BELL PEPPERS

Three servings

Here is a wonderful balanced seafood and pasta dish. Fresh scallops are available all year round but supplies are more plentiful in summertime. Try to use them in your cooking from late spring through early fall.

2 teaspoons butter
2 teaspoons canola oil
1 red bell pepper, julienned
3 tablespoons minced shallots
1/4 cup low-fat milk
13 ounces sea scallops
1/2 tablespoon flour
Salt and pepper
3 cups hot cooked linguine
1/4 cup chopped fresh parsley

▶ In a skillet melt the butter and oil over medium heat. Add the bell peppers and shallots. Sauté for 1 to 2 minutes, or until the peppers are soft. Increase the heat to medium-high and add the milk. Bring the mixture to a boil, stirring continually.

▶ Coat the scallops well with the flour. Reduce the heat to medium and add them to the skillet. Cook until they are opaque, stirring frequently, about 1 minute. Season with salt and pepper. Toss the cooked pasta with half the sauce and parsley in a large bowl. Transfer to a serving plate and top with the scallops and remaining sauce.

One third of this recipe equals 1 serving.

BLOCKS PER SERVING:	
CARBS:	4
PROTEIN:	4
FAT:	4

PENNE WITH SCALLOPS IN A TOMATO-VODKA SAUCE

Four servings

This tasty combination of basil, rosemary, tomatoes, and vodka is great with scallops. It makes an excellent sauce for other seafood as well, such as salmon steaks.

16 ounces sea scallops
3 teaspoons olive oil
1 teaspoon butter
1 can (15 ounces) Italian-style stewed tomatoes
$1/4$ teaspoon crushed dried rosemary
3 tablespoons minced fresh basil
Salt and pepper
$1/4$ cup vodka
1 teaspoon whipping cream
$2^{1}/_{2}$ hot cooked penne
$1/4$ cup chopped fresh parsley

▶ In a large skillet, sauté the scallops in the oil over medium heat until they are translucent, about 1 minute. Remove them with a slotted spoon and set aside.

▶ Melt the butter in the same skillet over medium heat. Add the tomatoes and rosemary, bring to a boil, crushing the tomatoes with the back of a spoon. Reduce the heat to low and add the basil. Simmer for 10 minutes. Season with salt and pepper. Increase the heat to medium. Add the vodka and cream. Bring to a simmer and cook for 3 to 4 minutes. Add the scallops and simmer until heated through, stirring occasionally, about 3 minutes. Add the pasta to the sauce in the skillet and stir. Mix in the parsley and serve immediately. Make up the missing carbohydrate blocks for 1 person with 2 cups tossed salad on the side.

One fourth of this recipe equals 1 serving.

BLOCKS PER SERVING:	
CARBS:	3
PROTEIN:	4
FAT:	4

SCALLOP-VEGETABLE STIR-FRY WITH AN OYSTER SAUCE

Four servings

Bay scallops come about 100 to the pound. Look for nice white, sweet smelling ones.

1 cup vegetable stock (page 14)
2 tablespoons oyster sauce
1 tablespoon cornstarch
$\frac{1}{2}$ scant teaspoon dark sesame oil, divided (page 11)
1 tablespoon canola oil
1 carrot, sliced
1 cup sliced mushrooms
1 cup snow peas, stringed
3 scallions, green parts only, chopped
1 tablespoon minced fresh ginger
1 pound fresh sea scallops, cut in half
Soy sauce

► Combine the vegetable stock, oyster sauce, cornstarch, and sesame oil. Let stand for 15 minutes.

► Heat half the oil in a wok or heavy skillet over medium heat. Add the carrots and stir-fry for 4 to 5 minutes or until they are soft. Add the mushrooms and stir-fry for 1 minute. Add the snow peas and stir-fry for 2 minutes, or until they are bright green. Transfer the vegetables to a bowl.

► Add the remaining oil to the wok. Add the scallions and ginger. Stir-fry until aromatic, about 1 minute. Add the scallops and stir-fry for 2 minutes. Whip the oyster sauce mixture to make sure the cornstarch has dissolved and add to the wok. Stir until the sauce has thickened. Return the vegetables to the wok and stir until everything is well coated with the sauce. Serve with soy sauce if desired. Make up the missing carbohydrate blocks for 1 person with $\frac{1}{4}$ cup steamed rice on the side.

BLOCKS PER SERVING:	
CARBS:	2
PROTEIN:	3
FAT:	3

One fourth of this recipe equals 1 serving.

SEARED SEA SCALLOPS WITH SAFFRON

Six servings

Obviously I really like to cook with scallops. This great dish shows off how good a balanced meal can be.

1¹/₂ pounds sea scallops
Salt and pepper
¹/₂ tablespoon olive oil, divided
3 pinches crumbled saffron, divided
¹/₂ tablespoon butter
2 tablespoons chopped shallots
1 tablespoon dry vermouth
1 tablespoon dry white wine
¹/₃ cup vegetable stock (page 14)
2 tablespoons whipping cream

► Season the scallops with salt and pepper. Heat half the oil in a skillet over medium heat. Add 1 pinch of saffron and stir for 30 seconds. Arrange half the scallops in the skillet. Cook from 1 to 2 minutes on each side until golden and just cooked through. Transfer the scallops to a plate and keep warm. Wipe the skillet clean, and repeat procedure with the remaining scallops.

► Without cleaning the skillet, melt the butter over reduced heat and stir in the shallots and remaining saffron. Cook until softened. Add the vermouth and wine. Cook for 3 minutes scraping up any brown bits. Increase the heat to medium. Add the stock and cook until reduced by half. Add the cream and juices that have accumulated on the scallop plate. Cook until reduced by about a half again. Season the saffron cream with salt and pepper and pour over the scallops. Make up the missing carbohydrate blocks for 1 person with 1 cup cooked black beans or lentils on the side.

One sixth of this recipe equals 1 serving.

BLOCKS PER SERVING:	
CARBS:	¹/₂
PROTEIN:	5
FAT:	5

SNACKS

This was the hardest section of the book for me to write. What is a snack anyway? Often for me it's leftover dinner or lunch. Most of the time I'm happy with a commercial balanced candy bar.

The snack probably is the most important component of the balanced meal plan. Remember to eat a snack in the afternoon and evening, even when you're not hungry!

I tend to think of my evening snack as an extension of dinner. It is at snack time that I have my dessert. So I have added many sweets in this section. I found that when baking, there is no substitute for real ingredients like butter and sugar. I've seen lots of balanced recipes for desserts calling for fructose instead of sugar. Some research has led me to believe that fructose is probably harmful for human consumption, and for that reason I've elected to stay away from it. Also, fructose tends to lose some sweetness when cooked. So even though a balanced recipe allows you to use more, you end up with a less desirable product.

Egg substitutes seem to work well in most baked goods, and so I use them extensively. Also there doesn't seem to be too much difference in performance between protein powder and whey powder, but I prefer the whey which has more protein per tablespoon than the protein powder. I also think it tastes better.

Several good commercial balanced candy bars are on the market. They are balanced at 2 blocks each, and range in price and flavor. There are a couple I like a lot. You may want to check them out. Having a box or two of these lying around can make snack time a no-brainer.

Some imitation balanced candy bars are starting to pop up that are actually high-protein bars. If you're not sure if a particular product is balanced, read the label.

FRESH HERB DIP WITH CRACKERS

Four servings

This zesty dip is great with crackers and chips. It is excellent with fresh raw vegetables as well.

1 garlic clove, chopped
1/4 cup minced fresh parsley
1 tablespoon minced fresh dill
Pepper
1/2 cup low-fat yogurt
1/2 cup low-fat cottage cheese
2 tablespoons prepared horseradish
16 Saltines

▶ Combine all the ingredients except the crackers in a food processor or blender. Blend until smooth and creamy. Cover and chill for two hours. Top each cracker with 1/2 tablespoon dip. Makes about 1 cup.

Four crackers with topping equals 1 serving.

BLOCKS PER SERVING:	
CARBS:	1
PROTEIN:	1
FAT:	1

CURRY DIP WITH CRACKERS

Four servings

This dip is plenty spicy. If you want it more so, add some cayenne or hot paprika.

   3 scallions, chopped
   1½ scant teaspoons butter
   1 tablespoon curry powder
   1 cup low-fat yogurt
   2 tablespoons protein powder
   1 tablespoon finely chopped golden raisins
   Pepper (optional)
   16 Saltines

▶ Melt the butter in a small skillet over low heat. Sauté the scallions until soft. Add the curry powder and mix well. Remove the skillet from the heat and stir the mixture into the yogurt with the protein powder. Add the raisins and pepper if desired. Cover and chill for 2 hours. Top each cracker with ¾ of a tablespoon of dip. Makes about 1½ cups.

Four crackers with topping equals 1 serving.

BLOCKS PER SERVING:	
CARBS:	1
PROTEIN:	1
FAT:	1

GINGER TOFU DIP WITH CRACKERS

Four servings

This creamy dip has a wonderful fresh ginger taste.

- 1 tablespoon minced fresh ginger
- 2 scallions, chopped
- 2 cloves garlic, minced
- 2 tablespoons low-sodium soy sauce
- 1 teaspoon light sesame oil (page 11)
- 1 scant teaspoon melted butter
- 1½ cups soft tofu, drained
- 16 Saltines

▶ Combine all the ingredients except the crackers in a food processor or blender and process until smooth and creamy. Cover and chill for at least 2 hours. Top each cracker with ¾ tablespoon dip. Makes about 1½ cups.

Four crackers with topping equals 1 serving.

BLOCKS PER SERVING:	
CARBS:	1
PROTEIN:	1
FAT:	1

AVOCADO AND CRABMEAT DIP ON RYE BREAD

Four servings

The crabmeat and avocado make a perfect marriage in this balanced snack.

1/4 avocado, mashed
6 ounces crabmeat, shredded
1 tablespoon low-fat yogurt
1/2 tablespoon light canola mayonnaise
1/2 teaspoon pepper
1/2 teaspoon lemon zest
1/2 teaspoon fresh lemon juice
4 slices firm rye bread
Fresh alfalfa sprouts

▶ In a bowl, mix together the avocado, crabmeat, yogurt, mayonnaise, pepper, lemon zest, and lemon juice. Mix well. Cut the bread slices into 16 squares. Top each square with a tablespoon of the crab mixture. Top the crab mixture with a good pinch of alfalfa sprouts. Each square is equal to about 1/4 block carbohydrate, protein, and fat.

Four crackers with topping equals 1 serving.

BLOCKS PER SERVING:	
CARBS:	1
PROTEIN:	1
FAT:	1

SPICY AVOCADO GRILLED CHEESE

Four servings

Here is an unusual, open-faced version of a classic sandwich. Cut each bread slice in half for a snack or eat both slices for lunch.

> 1 tablespoon mashed avocado
> Salt and pepper
> 1/8 teaspoon cayenne
> 1/8 teaspoon dill
> 1/8 teaspoon lemon juice
> 3 teaspoon light canola mayonnaise
> 2 slices whole wheat bread, toasted
> 1 tablespoon drained and thinly sliced canned jalapeño
> pepper
> 4 tomato slices
> 4 ounces Monterey Jack cheese, thinly sliced
> 1/2 cup alfalfa sprouts

▶ Preheat the broiler.

▶ In a bowl, mix the avocado, salt, pepper, cayenne, dill, lemon juice, and mayonnaise until smooth and creamy. Spread the avocado evenly on the toast. Add the peppers, and tomato, and cover with the cheese. Place under the broiler, about 6 inches from the flame for 2 to 3 minutes, or until the cheese has just started to melt. Remove from the oven, top with the sprouts, cut each piece in half, and serve.

One half slice of bread with topping equals 1 serving.

BLOCKS PER SERVING:	
CARBS:	1
PROTEIN:	1
FAT:	1

ROASTED PEPPERS ON CROISSANT

Two servings

This recipe makes a perfectly balanced snack that is pretty to look at.

1 red bell pepper, roasted and diced
1 yellow bell pepper, roasted and diced
3 teaspoons light canola mayonnaise
1 scant teaspoon olive oil
$\frac{1}{2}$ teaspoon dried basil
Salt and pepper
$\frac{1}{2}$ cup grated Parmesan cheese
1 mini croissant, sliced in half

▶ Preheat the broiler.

▶ In a bowl, mix the mayonnaise, oil, basil, salt, and pepper until smooth and creamy. Stir in the bell peppers. Top each croissant half with half the bell pepper spread. Sprinkle the cheese over the top and place in the broiler about 6 inches from the heat. Broil for 2 to 3 minutes, or until the cheese starts to melt. Remove from the oven and serve.

One half a mini croissant with topping equals 1 serving.

BLOCKS PER SERVING:	
CARBS:	2
PROTEIN:	2
FAT:	2

TOFU PITAS

Two servings

1 teaspoon Dijon-style mustard
1 tablespoon light canola mayonnaise
$1/2$ tablespoon white wine vinegar
$1/4$ teaspoon curry powder
$1/4$ teaspoon cumin
Salt and pepper
$1/2$ cup firm low-fat tofu, diced
$1/2$ scallion, chopped fine
1 tablespoon finely chopped red bell pepper
$1/2$ whole wheat mini pita
$1/2$ cup lettuce, shredded
1 tablespoon tomato, chopped
2 teaspoons bacon bits

▶ In a food processor or blender, combine the mustard, mayonnaise, vinegar, curry, cumin, salt and pepper. Blend until creamy, about 30 seconds. Transfer to a small bowl and stir in the tofu, scallion, and bell pepper.

▶ Let stand for 5 to 10 minutes. Stuff the pita pocket with the mixture, top with the lettuce, tomato, and bacon bits. Cut in half.

One quarter mini pita with topping equals 1 serving.

BLOCKS PER SERVING:	
CARBS:	$1^1/2$
PROTEIN:	$1^1/2$
FAT:	$1^1/2$

EASY BAKED POLENTA

Nine servings

The scallion and fresh parsley gives this simple polenta dish a fresh garden flavor.

1 cup low-fat chicken stock
¼ cup instant polenta
2 tablespoons protein powder
¼ teaspoon salt
Pinch pepper
1 tablespoon chopped fresh parsley
1 scallion, white part only, minced
2 teaspoons melted butter
3 tablespoons grated Parmesan cheese
Cooking spray

▶ Preheat the oven broiler.

▶ Coat a 9x9-inch baking dish with cooking spray.

▶ In a medium saucepan, bring the chicken stock to a boil. Mix the polenta with the protein powder, salt, and pepper. Add to the boiling chicken stock, stirring constantly. Cook and stir the polenta for about 15 minutes, or until it starts to pull away from the sides of the pan. Remove from the heat and stir in the parsley and onions. Pour the warm polenta into the prepared pan and let cool.

▶ Paint the top of the polenta with melted butter and put it in the broiler about 6 inches from the heat. Broil for several minutes, until the top turns golden and the butter is bubbling. Remove from the oven and sprinkle the cheese evenly over the top. Let stand in the baking dish on a rack to cool. Cut into nine squares.

One polenta square equals 1 serving.

BLOCKS PER SERVING:	
CARBS:	½
PROTEIN:	1
FAT:	1

TURKEY DIM SUM

15 servings

I find dim sum a hassle to make, so I make a lot by doubling the recipe. You can freeze the ones you don't use for up to 2 months.

6 dried shiitake mushrooms
1 pound ground turkey
1 tablespoon light sesame oil
1/3 cup finely chopped scallion
1 tablespoon minced fresh parsley
1 tablespoon minced fresh ginger
1/2 cup water chestnuts, finely chopped
1/2 cup bamboo shoots, finely chopped
2 tablespoons low-sodium soy sauce
1 egg white
1 tablespoon cornstarch
1 tablespoon protein powder
1 tablespoon chopped slivered almonds
30 round wonton wrappers (1/2 package)

▶ Soak the dried mushrooms in warm water for 20 minutes until soft. Remove the stems and mince. In a skillet over medium heat brown the turkey meat with the oil. Combine the mushrooms and the rest of the ingredients with the turkey and mix well.

▶ With your fingers, lightly dampen the edge of the dim sum wrapper. Place a tablespoon of the filling in the center of each wrapper. Gather up the sides around the filling and press together. Seal the sides up around the filling leaving a small opening at the top. Gently squeeze the skin against the filling and flatten out the bottom.

▶ You can make a homemade steamer by placing parchment paper over a rack set in a large skillet. Place the dim sum on the parchment paper in the bottom of a steamer. Cover and steam over boiling water for 20 minutes. Makes about 30 small dim sum.

BLOCKS PER SERVING:	
CARBS:	1
PROTEIN:	1
FAT:	1

Two dim sum equals 1 serving.

SHRIMP AND SCALLOP DIM SUM

— ❦ —

15 servings

The shrimp and scallop combination makes a wonderful dim sum filling.

$^3/_4$ **pound shrimp, peeled, deveined, and minced**
$^1/_2$ **pound scallops, minced**
$^1/_3$ **cup finely chopped bamboo shoots**
$^1/_3$ **cup finely chopped water chestnuts**
$^1/_4$ **teaspoon red pepper flakes**
$^1/_4$ **teaspoon five-spice powder**
2 teaspoons minced fresh parsley
30 square dim sum wrappers ($^1/_2$ package)

▶ Combine all the ingredients, except the wrappers, in a large bowl and mix well.

▶ With your fingers lightly dampen the edges of the dim sum wrapper. Place 1 tablespoon filling along the bottom in the center. Roll once and tuck in the sides of the wrapper. Continue rolling to form a tight package. Repeat with the remaining dim sum wrappers.

▶ Place the dumplings, seam side down, on a piece of parchment paper in the bottom of a steamer. (A homemade steamer can be made by placing parchment paper on a rack inside a large skillet.) Cover and steam over boiling water for 15 minutes. Makes about 30 dim sum.

Two dim sum equals 1 serving.

BLOCKS PER SERVING:	
CARBS:	1
PROTEIN:	1
FAT:	1

ARTICHOKES WITH A
TARRAGON-MUSTARD SAUCE

Four servings

This sauce, with a mild lemon flavor that tastes like a creamy Hollandaise sauce, is a perfect accompaniment for artichokes.

4 small artichokes, outer leaves removed
1 tablespoon balsamic vinegar
4 tablespoons low-fat sour cream
1 cup low-fat cottage cheese
1$\frac{1}{2}$ tablespoons fresh lemon juice
$\frac{1}{8}$ teaspoon salt
$\frac{1}{4}$ teaspoon pepper
$\frac{1}{2}$ teaspoon tarragon
2 teaspoons Dijon-style mustard

▶ Bring a large pot of water to boil on the top of the stove. Add the artichokes and the vinegar. When the water begins to boil again, reduce to a simmer and cook for 30 minutes. Drain and cool.

▶ In a bowl, combine the sour cream, cottage cheese, lemon juice, salt, pepper, tarragon, and mustard. With a wire whisk, beat until smooth. Cut the artichokes in half. Remove the choke. Serve the four halves with a tablespoon of sauce on the side.

One artichoke with sauce equals 1 serving.

BLOCKS PER SERVING:	
CARBS:	2
PROTEIN:	2
FAT:	2

MELON AND LOX

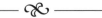

Two servings

This balanced snack is a clever blend of sweet, salty, and tangy flavors.

$^1/_2$ **honeydew melon, peeled and sliced**
6 ounces lox, thinly sliced
Fresh ground pepper
4 teaspoons "Philly Free" cream cheese, softened
1 tablespoon chopped fresh chives
2 lemon wedges

▶ Divide the melon slices between two plates. Top with the lox slices, or wrap them around the melon. Season with the pepper.

▶ In a small bowl, combine the cream cheese and chives. Mix well. Top each melon slice with the cream cheese mixture. Squeeze on a little lemon juice.

One half this recipe equals 1 serving.

BLOCKS PER SERVING:	
CARBS:	2
PROTEIN:	2
FAT:	2

CHIVE POPOVERS

Twelve servings

These popovers are good at room temperature but great right out of the oven.

Cooking spray
2 eggs
2 scant teaspoons olive oil
1/2 cup all-purpose flour
2 tablespoons whey protein
1/4 teaspoon salt
Pepper
1 cup 1% milk
1/4 cup finely cut fresh chives

▶ Preheat the oven to 400° F.

▶ Coat eight muffin cups with the cooking spray.

▶ In a food processor or blender, combine the eggs, oil, flour, whey protein, salt, and pepper. Blend for about 30 seconds. With the machine running pour in the milk and blend until smooth. Stir in the chives. Divide the batter among the muffin cups filling no more than 1/4-inch from the rim. Bake for 40 minutes without opening the oven door. Turn off the oven and slit each popover with a knife. Return them to the oven and let them sit for an additional 5 to 10 minutes. Turn out onto a rack. Makes 12 muffins.

One muffin equals 1 serving.

BLOCKS PER SERVING:	
CARBS:	1/2
PROTEIN:	1/2
FAT:	1/2

ALMOND SUGAR COOKIES

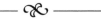

Twenty servings

These crisp cookies make a great snack idea. You should keep lots around.

2 tablespoons almond butter
2 tablespoons canola oil
3 tablespoons sugar
1 egg white, beaten
1 teaspoon almond extract
1 teaspoon vanilla extract
¾ cup all-purpose flour
2 tablespoons whey protein
⅛ teaspoon baking soda
¼ teaspoon salt
⅛ teaspoon cream of tartar
32 almond slices

▶ Preheat the oven to 350° F.

▶ In a small bowl, cream the almond butter and oil until smooth. Add the sugar and beat until light and fluffy. Mix in the egg white and extracts.

▶ In another bowl, combine the flour, whey protein, baking soda, salt, and cream of tartar. Slowly stir the flour mixture into the almond butter mixture and mix well.

▶ Put the dough between to sheets of wax paper and flatten with your hand. With a rolling pin, roll the dough out about ¼-inch thick. Using a 2-inch round cookie cutter, cut out 20 cookies. Top each cookie with an almond slice. Bake on a cookie sheet for 8 to 10 minutes, until lightly browned. Transfer to a flat surface to cool.

One cookie equals 1 serving.

BLOCKS PER SERVING:	
CARBS:	1
PROTEIN:	1
FAT:	1

OATMEAL-RAISIN COOKIES

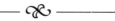

Thirty servings

Of all the balanced cookie recipes I've seen, I like these oatmeal cookies the best.

1¹/₂ cups rolled oats
¹/₂ cup all-purpose flour
1 tablespoons whey protein
¹/₂ teaspoon baking soda
¹/₄ teaspoon salt
1 tablespoon sugar
2 egg whites
3 tablespoons peach juice concentrate
¹/₄ cup almond butter
1 teaspoon almond extract
4 tablespoons chopped raisins
Cooking spray

▶ Preheat the oven to 375° F.

▶ In a bowl, combine the oats, flour, whey protein, baking soda, salt, and sugar. In another bowl, whip the egg whites, peach juice, almond butter, almond extract, and raisins together until well combined. Combine the two mixtures and stir until blended. Drop by rounded tablespoonfuls onto a baking sheet lightly coated with cooking spray. You should have 30 cookies. With the cooking spray, lightly coat the bottom of a glass, dip in additional sugar, and flatten the cookies. Bake for 8 minutes, or until lightly browned. Let sit on the baking sheet for a minute or two, then transfer to a flat surface to cool.

One cookie equals 1 serving.

BLOCKS PER SERVING:	
CARBS:	¹/₂
PROTEIN:	¹/₂
FAT:	¹/₂

PEANUT BUTTER-OATMEAL COOKIES

Thirty servings

The peanut butter and oatmeal make a great tasting combination in these balanced cookies.

1¹⁄₂ cups rolled oats
¹⁄₂ cup all-purpose flour
3 tablespoons whey protein
¹⁄₂ teaspoon baking powder
¹⁄₄ teaspoon salt
2¹⁄₂ teaspoons sugar
3 tablespoons 1% milk
2 egg whites
1 teaspoon vanilla extract
¹⁄₂ cup creamy or chunky peanut butter
Cooking spray

▶ Preheat the oven to 350° F.

▶ In a large bowl, combine the oats, flour, whey protein, baking powder, and salt. Set aside.

▶ In another bowl, mix the sugar, milk, egg white, vanilla, and peanut butter until smooth and creamy. Combine the two mixtures and stir and knead until well blended.

▶ Coat a baking sheet with the cooking spray and drop the batter onto the sheet by the tablespoonful about 1¹⁄₂ inches apart. You should have 30 cookies. Coat the bottom of a glass with cooking spray, dip it in additional sugar, and flatten the cookies. Bake for 8 to 10 minutes or until the cookies just turn light brown.

One cookie equals 1 serving.

BLOCKS PER SERVING:	
CARBS:	1
PROTEIN:	1
FAT:	1

SPICE COOKIES

Twenty-four servings

If you are good and follow the recipe, you will have balanced cookies. I must confess that I usually cheat and throw in a table-spoon or two of extra sugar. I like my baked goods a little on the sweet side.

> **2 tablespoons almond butter**
> **3 tablespoons molasses**
> **2 egg whites**
> **$1/2$ teaspoon almond extract**
> **$1^1/2$ cups oats**
> **$1/2$ cup all-purpose flour**
> **3 tablespoons whey protein**
> **$1/2$ teaspoon baking soda**
> **$1/4$ teaspoon salt**
> **$1/2$ teaspoon cinnamon**
> **$1/4$ teaspoon nutmeg**
> **Cooking spray**

▶ Preheat the oven to 350° F.

▶ In a large bowl mix the almond butter with the molasses. Add the egg whites one at a time, mixing well after each addition. Add the almond extract.

▶ In another bowl, combine the oats, flour, whey protein, baking soda, salt, cinnamon, and nutmeg. Mix well and add the molasses mixture. Combine the two.

▶ Spray a baking sheet with the cooking spray. Drop the batter onto the baking sheet by the tablespoonful, about $1^1/2$ inches apart. You should have 24 cookies. Bake for 8 to 10 minutes, or until the cookies start to brown on top. Remove from the oven and cool on a flat surface.

One cookie equals 1 serving.

BLOCKS PER SERVING:	
CARBS:	$1/2$
PROTEIN:	$1/2$
FAT:	$1/2$

CAPPUCCINO MOUSSE

Eight servings

Just when you thought the days for chocolate mousse for dessert were over, here's a balanced snack you'll love.

2 teaspoons unflavored gelatin
$\frac{1}{2}$ cup plus 2 tablespoons 1% milk
1 ounce semisweet chocolate, grated
1 teaspoon instant espresso coffee grains
2 tablespoons vanilla protein powder
1 teaspoon vanilla extract
2 cups ice cubes
1 cup cold water
6 egg whites
1 tablespoon sugar
$\frac{1}{2}$ cup frozen whipped topping mix, thawed

▶ In a saucepan, sprinkle the gelatin over the milk and let it stand for 1 minute to soften. Cook over medium heat, stirring constantly until the gelatin is dissolved. Add the chocolate, espresso powder, protein powder, and vanilla. Cook and stir until the chocolate has melted.

▶ In a large bowl, mix the ice cubes with the cold water. Transfer the chocolate mixture to a smaller bowl, set it in the ice water, and let stand. Stir frequently until the mixture has cooled to the touch.

▶ In a mixing bowl, beat the egg whites until soft peaks start to form. Slowly add the sugar while beating. Set aside.

▶ Remove the chocolate from the ice water and stir in half of the whipped topping until well blended. Fold in the other half. Then slowly fold in the beaten egg whites. Divide the mousse into eight $\frac{1}{2}$-cup individual serving dishes, cover, and chill overnight.

One half cup of mousse equals 1 serving.

BLOCKS PER SERVING:	
CARBS:	1
PROTEIN:	1
FAT:	1

CRUSTLESS PUMPKIN PIE

Eight servings

You can bake this pie in a pastry shell. But the crust will add one block per slice to the carbohydrate and fat count.

$1/4$ cup egg substitute
2 egg whites
$1^1/_2$ cups soft or whipped tofu
3 tablespoons whey protein
2 cups (canned) non-sweetened pumpkin
$1/4$ cup brown sugar
2 tablespoons molasses
1 teaspoon cinnamon
$1^1/_2$ teaspoons pumpkin pie spice
$1/2$ teaspoon salt
Cooking spray

▶ Preheat the oven to 325° F.

▶ In a food processor or blender, mix all the ingredients together until smooth and creamy. Coat a 9-inch pie pan with cooking spray and pour the mixture into the pan. Bake for 45 to 60 minutes, or until a knife inserted into the middle comes out clean. Chill for 2 hours before serving. Makes 8 wedges.

One wedge of pie equals 1 serving.

BLOCKS PER SERVING:	
CARBS:	2
PROTEIN:	2
FAT:	2

CHOCOLATE PUDDING SNACK

Four servings

This fast make-ahead snack will keep for several days in the refrigerator. Be sure it is well covered.

2 cups non-fat milk
1 tablespoon instant espresso grains
1¼ cups non-fat cottage cheese
1 3-ounce box Jell-O American Tapioca Pudding
2 tablespoons chopped almonds

▶ In a blender or food processor, mix the milk, espresso, and cheese on low speed until smooth. Add the pudding mix and nuts. Blend until creamy. Pour into a bowl, cover, and refrigerate for 2 hours. Each ⅔ cup serving contains about 2 blocks carbohydrate, protein, and fat.

BLOCKS PER SERVING:	
CARBS:	2
PROTEIN:	2
FAT:	2

CHOCOLATE TOFU PUDDING SNACK

— ❧ —

Four servings

The tofu and almonds gives this pudding an interesting taste and texture. Try it for a change.

4 tablespoons blanched almonds
1^1/$_2$ cups tofu
^{1}/$_3$ cup cocoa powder
^{1}/$_4$ cup sugar
^{1}/$_2$ teaspoon vanilla extract

▶ Preheat the oven to 400° F.

▶ Line a baking sheet with tin foil and spread the almonds evenly on it. Bake for 7 to 10 minutes, or until lightly browned. Be careful they don't burn.

▶ Take them from the oven, let cool, and chop coarsely.

▶ In a food processor, combine the tofu, cocoa powder, sugar, and vanilla. Process until smooth. Transfer the pudding to a serving bowl. Sprinkle the nuts evenly over the top, cover, and refrigerate for several hours. A ^{2}/$_3$ cup serving contains about 2 blocks carbohydrate, protein, and fat.

BLOCKS PER SERVING:	
CARBS:	2
PROTEIN:	2
FAT:	2

BANANA-NUT MUFFINS

Eighteen servings

These muffins go well either as a snack or for a light breakfast.

1 cup whole wheat pastry flour
$^1/_4$ cup whey protein
2 tablespoons sugar
2 teaspoons baking powder
1 teaspoon baking soda
$^1/_2$ teaspoon salt
2 egg whites, beaten
$^1/_2$ cup 1% milk
1 tablespoon canola oil
1 ripe banana, mashed
$^1/_3$ cup water
Cooking spray

▶ Preheat the oven to 400° F.

▶ Combine the flour, whey protein, sugar, baking powder, baking soda, and salt in a large bowl. In another bowl, combine the egg whites, milk, oil, and mashed banana. Make a well in the center of the flour mixture and pour the banana mixture into it. Mix the ingredients together from the inside out. Add the water a little at a time until the dough reaches batter consistency.

▶ Lightly coat two muffin tins with the cooking spray or line with paper liners. Divide the batter among the muffin cups and bake for 25 minutes or until golden. Cool on a wire rack. Makes 18 muffins.

One muffin equals 1 serving.

BLOCKS PER SERVING:	
CARBS:	1
PROTEIN:	1
FAT:	1

ORANGE-GINGERBREAD MUFFINS

Eighteen servings

These muffins make great holiday balanced fare. Serve them warm for a special treat.

1 cup whole wheat pastry flour
$1/4$ cup sugar
9 tablespoons whey protein
$1^1/2$ teaspoons baking soda
$1/2$ teaspoon ground ginger
$1/2$ teaspoon ground cinnamon
$1/8$ teaspoon ground cloves
1 tablespoon orange zest
$3/4$ cup water
4 egg whites, lightly beaten
4 teaspoons almond butter
$1/4$ cup dark molasses
$1/4$ cup canola oil
Cooking spray

▶ Preheat the oven to 375° F.

▶ In a large bowl, combine the flour, sugar, whey protein, baking soda, ginger, cinnamon, cloves, and orange zest. In another bowl combine the water, egg white, almond butter, molasses, and oil and mix well. Make a well in the center of the flour mixture and pour the liquid mixture into the center. Mix ingredients together from the inside out.

▶ Spray two muffin tins with the cooking spray or line with paper liners. Divide the batter evenly among the muffin cups. Bake for 15 minutes or until a toothpick inserted into the center comes out clean. Remove from the oven and cool on a wire rack. Makes 18 muffins.

One muffin equals 1 serving.

BLOCKS PER SERVING:	
CARBS:	2
PROTEIN:	2
FAT:	2

PUMPKIN MUFFINS

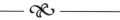

Twelve servings

6 tablespoons all-purpose flour
5 tablespoons whey protein
⅔ cup nonfat powdered milk
2 tablespoons sugar
1 teaspoon baking soda
2 teaspoons ground cinnamon
¼ teaspoon ground cloves
½ teaspoon ground allspice
½ teaspoon ground nutmeg
¼ teaspoon ground ginger
¼ teaspoon salt
½ can (15 ounces) pumpkin
1 tablespoon molasses
1 teaspoon vanilla
1½ tablespoons canola oil
4 egg whites, lightly beaten
⅓ cup water
Cooking spray

▶ Preheat the oven to 350° F.

▶ Combine the flour and other dry ingredients in a large bowl. In another bowl, mix together the pumpkin, molasses, vanilla, oil, and egg whites.

▶ Mix the dry ingredients with the pumpkin mixture. Add the water a little at a time until the dough reaches a batter consistency.

▶ Spray a muffin tin with the cooking spray. Divide the batter evenly among the muffin cups and bake for 10 to 15 minutes, or until a toothpick inserted into the middle comes out clean. Makes 12 muffins.

One muffin equals 1 serving.

BLOCKS PER SERVING:	
CARBS:	1
PROTEIN:	1
FAT:	1

BLUEBERRY MUFFINS

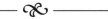

Twelve servings

Use fresh blueberries when they are in season for extra-tasty muffins.

- ¾ cup all-purpose flour
- ¼ cup wheat bran
- 2 tablespoons sugar
- 3 tablespoons whey protein
- 2 teaspoons baking powder
- 1 teaspoon baking soda
- ¼ teaspoon salt
- ¼ teaspoon ground cinnamon
- 1 cup 1% milk
- 2 egg whites, beaten
- 1 teaspoon vanilla extract
- 2 tablespoons canola oil
- ⅓ cup water
- ½ cup blueberries, fresh or frozen
- Cooking spray

▶ Preheat the oven to 350° F.

▶ In a large bowl, combine the flour, wheat bran, sugar, whey protein, baking powder, baking soda, salt, and cinnamon. In another bowl combine the milk, egg whites, vanilla extract, and oil. Make a well in the flour mixture and pour the milk mixture into the center. Mix the ingredients together from the inside out. Add the water to the dough a little at a time until it is batter consistency. Fold in the berries.

▶ Spray a muffin tin with the cooking spray or line with paper liners. Pour the batter into the muffin cups. Bake for 15 to 20 minutes, or until a toothpick inserted into the center comes out clean. Remove from the oven, and let sit for 5 minutes before serving. Makes 12 muffins.

One muffin equals 1 serving.

BLOCKS PER SERVING:	
CARBS:	1½
PROTEIN:	1½
FAT:	1½

BANANA BREAD

―――――――――― ∾ ――――――――――

Eighteen servings

The spices and almond flavoring in this recipe make this bread quite unusual.

2 very ripe bananas, mashed
$1/4$ cup canola oil
2 egg whites
$1/8$ teaspoon almond extract
2 tablespoons sugar
2 tablespoons warm water
$1/4$ cup whey protein
1 cup all-purpose flour
$1/4$ teaspoon ground nutmeg
$1/8$ teaspoon ground cloves
2 teaspoons baking powder
$1/4$ teaspoon baking soda
Cooking spray

▶ Preheat the oven to 350° F.

▶ In a bowl, combine the bananas, oil, egg whites, and almond extract. In a small bowl mix the sugar and water. Add the sugar-water to the banana mixture and mix well. Sift together the protein powder, flour, nutmeg, cloves, baking powder, and the baking soda. Slowly add the banana mixture to the dry ingredients until well blended. Do not overmix.

▶ Coat a 9x5-inch loaf pan with cooking spray and spread the batter in it. Bake for 50 to 60 minutes, or until golden brown and a toothpick inserted into the middle comes out clean. Cool in the pan for 5 minutes and then turn out onto a wire rack to continue cooling. Cut into 18 $1/2$-inch slices.

Each slice equals 1 serving.

BLOCKS PER SERVING:	
CARBS:	2
PROTEIN:	2
FAT:	2

BALANCED BROWNIES

Fourteen servings

No cookbook is complete without a brownie recipe. Here is my balanced version.

¹/₂ cup whole wheat pastry flour
4 tablespoons whey protein
¹/₂ cup unsweetened cocoa powder
¹/₂ teaspoon baking soda
¹/₄ teaspoon salt
¹/₄ cup sugar
¹/₄ cup almond butter
4 egg whites, lightly beaten
¹/₂ cup water
1¹/₂ teaspoons vanilla
Cooking spray

▶ Preheat the oven to 325° F.

▶ Line a 9x8-inch baking pan with parchment or wax paper, lightly spray the pan with cooking spray, and dust it with flour.

▶ In a large measuring cup or bowl, combine the flour, whey protein, cocoa powder, baking soda, and salt, and mix well. In a mixing bowl, cream the sugar and almond butter until smooth. Add the egg whites, water and vanilla, mixing until smooth and creamy. Stir the flour mixture into the almond butter mixture until smooth. Spread the mixture evenly over the bottom of the prepared pan and bake for 15 to 20 minutes, or until a tooth-pick inserted into the middle comes out just a little moist.

▶ Cool for 15 minutes on a wire rack. Run a knife around the outside of the brownies to loosen from the pan. Remove and cut into 14 bars.

Each brownie equals 1 serving.

BLOCKS PER SERVING:	
CARBS:	1
PROTEIN:	1
FAT:	1

HOMEMADE 40-30-30 BARS

Eight servings

Getting tired of those high-priced balanced candy bars in the health food stores? Make your own at home for a fraction of the cost.

> ¼ cup blanched almonds
> ¼ cup sugar
> ¼ cup rolled oats
> ¼ cup whey protein
> 1 tablespoon cocoa powder (optional)
> Water

▶ Preheat the oven to 400° F.

▶ Line a baking sheet with tin foil. Spread the almonds out evenly and bake for 7 to 10 minutes until the almonds are brown. Watch that they do not burn.

▶ Pulse in a food processor until finely chopped.

▶ In a small saucepan, dissolve the sugar in about ½ cup water over low heat. Remove from the stove, add the almonds, and stir. Transfer the almond mixture to a large mixing bowl and add the oats. Start kneading the mixture with your hands and slowly add the whey protein. As the dough gets stiffer, add a little water and keep kneading. Continue to knead and add water until the dough has reached the right consistency, about the same as stiff bread dough. Roll the dough into a log. Or put it between two sheets of wax paper and roll it out with a rolling pin into a sheet about ½-inch thick.

▶ Refrigerate for 2 hours. Cut the dough into 8 equal pieces. Individually wrap and return to the refrigerator.

Each bar equals 1 serving.

BLOCKS PER SERVING:	
CARBS:	1½
PROTEIN:	1½
FAT:	1½

ONE-BLOCK SNACKS

Here are some great one-block snack ideas. Mix and match these food combinations any way, depending on what you feel like eating. Or you can save time by eating ½ of any balanced candy bar.

Carbohydrate	Protein	Fat
1 cup fresh strawberries	1 ounce favorite low-fat cheese	3 almonds
½ apple	1 ounce string cheese	7 peanuts, dry roasted
4 crackers	½ ounce beef jerky	1 tablespoon "lite" sour cream
¼ bagel	1 ½ ounce lox	½ tablespoon mashed avocado
½ cup blackberries	¼ cup cottage cheese	3 cashews, dry roasted
	½ cup flavored yogurt	1 macadamia nut, dry roasted

RELATED BOOKS BY THE CROSSING PRESS

Homestyle Mexican Cooking
By Lourdes Nichols

This tantalizing collection of over 180 authentic recipes from Mexican cuisine includes meat and poultry dishes, vegetables, salads, desserts, and drinks.

$16.95 * Paper * ISBN 0-89594-861-3

Homestyle Middle Eastern Cooking
By Pat Chapman

This collection of authentic recipes features spicy regional dishes selected from hundreds of recipes the author collected on his travels throughout the Middle East.

* $16.95 * Paper * ISBN 0-89594-860-5

Homestyle Thai and Indonesian Cooking
by Sri Owen

Sri Owen offers authentic recipes for sates, curries, fragrant rice dishes, spicy vegetables, and snacks and sweets. Includes adaptations using Western ingredients.

$16.95 * Paper * ISBN 0-89594-859-1

Homestyle Italian Cooking
By Lori Carangelo

These wonderful dishes use fresh ingredients, carefully prepared to bring out the special flavors of the best, homemade Italian cooking.

$16.95 * Paper * ISBN 0-89594-867-2

Cooking the Fat-free, Salt-free, Sugar-free Flavorful Way
by Marcia Sabate Williams

Based on the Pritikin Diet, this book is a collection of delectable recipes developed by the author to meet the special needs of her family. Williams utilizes traditional Creole seasoning to enhance the flavor of everything from breakfast to sauces, soups, dinners, and desserts.

$22.95 * Paper * ISBN 0-89594-858-3

To receive a current catalog from The Crossing Press
please call toll-free, 800-777-1048.
Visit our Web site on the Internet: www. crossingpress.com